Your Hidden Light
By Raana Zia
Published 2017 by The Light Network
Copyright © Raana Zia

Printed in the United States

Edited by Keidi Keating

ISBN: 978-0-9975727-4-2

Your Hidden Light

A Personal Guide to Creating Your Desired Life

By Raana Zia

This book is dedicated to…

My two amazing children, Aydin and Samar Latif,

Who inspire me, teach me, and bring joy to my life

Contents

Acknowledgements

I would like to thank the people in my life who have supported, helped, and inspired me in my growth journey and in the writing of this book.

First of all, I would like to thank my parents, Sultan and Farhana Zia, who have always prioritized their relationship with their children over anything. I am deeply grateful for their understanding and open-mindedness towards my process of self-discovery and self-realization. I know it isn't easy at times to understand why I have chosen a path that has taken me beyond the beliefs and norms of my heritage and upbringing, but it is because of their love that I have felt the freedom to be me.

Thank you to my husband, Nomaan Latif, who is my partner in life. His trust and belief in me has given me the foundational support I needed to follow this new path and complete this book. I am grateful and inspired by his open-mindedness and desire to learn and grow in new ways. Thank you to my children, Aydin and Samar Latif, who teach me new things all the time, and who are my purpose and inspiration for writing this book.

Thank you to Trudy Simmons who has been my personal coach along my journey, which finally led to the writing of this book. Her intuitive and coaching skills have always been right on in understanding what I needed to hear at that moment. Thank you to my friend Rebecca Kittle for all her encouragement, feedback, friendship, and inspiration. And thank you to Keidi Keating, my editor, who added love and light to this book.

Introduction

Your Hidden Light is meant to be a simple handbook that directly synthesizes the how, what, and why related to the power you have to create your reality. This book is a reflection of my many years of research, application, and personal self-discovery. I was searching for my true purpose and passion, a way to evolve my career, and greatly enhance my material life. Instead, I discovered so much more. I discovered we, as humans, are far more than our physical limited selves, and that our true nature is much more powerful than I had ever known. I learned that spirituality did not mean giving up material things, but that everything in the material world is created by what we cannot see. I experienced that by connecting with my true nature or my spiritual/soul self, I have the power to easily create anything I truly desire, and live a more positive and purposeful life. In fact, our purpose here is to create, grow, and evolve.

I grew up in what I consider to be a normal upper middle-class family in the state of Massachusetts. I am the daughter of Indian, Muslim immigrants who came to this country in the 1960s. My father is a retired corporate executive from the technology industry, and my mother is an author and a retired elementary school teacher. My parents have always been there to help, encourage, and guide both me and my older brother. I am very grateful to have such loving parents. With my cultural up-bringing, I was always expected to do well in school and go into a professional job after college. When I graduated from college, I took my first job in finance working for a bank. I have made a couple of industry changes since then, but I always stayed within the finance function. After I met my husband and got married, I really started to focus on growing my career. I began working for a big apparel retailer in their corporate office and quickly started to love the influence the finance function had in driving the business. I loved what I did and I was good at it. As a result, I continued to climb the corporate ladder. I ultimately reached my goal of becoming a chief financial officer and a member of an executive leadership team. When this milestone happened in my career, I was astonished because it fit exactly what I wanted. I had been clear in my head on what I wanted to do (be on an executive leadership team), in what industry (specialty retail), and where I wanted to move (the New York area). This opportunity fit all my desires, and I couldn't believe it was happening so fast. From a career progression stand-point I was receiving a double promotion within a year's time. It seemed unbelievable to me that I got exactly what I wanted, and I felt extremely grateful. I had to reflect on what was happening to me, and I knew the Universe was clearly showing me my power. I knew I had created this for myself, and this was not only good luck. A strong sense came over me that if I could achieve this, then I could achieve whatever I wanted in my career. The problem was, I didn't know what I really wanted. I had been so focused on the same career path for such a long time that I had never really taken the time to think about my real purpose in this lifetime. Something inside of me was pushing me to figure it out.

For the next few years I did a great deal of personal development work. I knew I needed to do this in order to make a dramatic shift in my career. I needed to figure out what my real purpose was and then believe I could achieve it. I needed a vision and I needed to believe in this vision. Looking back on my career, I knew I was able to accomplish my achievements because I had a vision and a belief in myself. It came naturally to me. I now wanted to do something that seemed unnatural, so I knew I had some work to do. I read many books, went to seminars and workshops, and worked with coaches. I wanted to break down my old belief systems that told me I could never create an independent career, that I was not smart enough, or that I was not an entrepreneur, and so on. I knew I needed to do these things first, but I really did not understand why. I was determined to understand why and how things in my life worked.

In my search for answers, I initially shied away from purely spiritual books. I was looking to enhance my material world and I was afraid that by reading spiritual books I would be told not to focus on material things. However, the more I wanted to understand the truth of who I was and how the world worked, the more I was pointed to the spiritual world. I had to open myself up to the unknown and unseen, and when I did life became much more interesting and exciting. My life started to make more sense and things became easier. I started to finally wake up.

I believe there are several different paths on our life's journey, and some are more strenuous than others. I am a firm believer that there is always an easier way that is lighter and minimizes the strain or effort – a more efficient, effective, and smarter way to do things. In my career, this was especially true for me. As a finance executive, my job was to drive efficiency and create effective teams that supported maximizing the company's profitability, so I was always looking for better ways to get things done. This way of being helped me to achieve my goals in the workplace in a way that minimized my stress and allowed me to have more fun. I knew if I wanted to make a change in my life or even enhance my life, there was a more direct way to go about it – a way that minimized the struggle, maximized my true abilities, and created more joy. What I discovered was exactly that.

I was not taught how to create efficiency or effectiveness in the workplace by my parents or in school. I learned through my own experiences. Similarly, I was not taught how to create an "efficient" life or a path of least resistance by my parents, schools, or religious institutions. It was my belief and my desire that brought me to this knowledge, and it was my experiences that made me understand the truth. The more I experienced myself creating my reality, the more committed I became to consciously doing this more often. Even now, when I find myself in an experience I do not like, I am committed to changing my internal compass to minimize the current suffering and create something new that serves me. I believe that the more you begin to understand and experience your power to create your experiences, the more you will prioritize and invest in growing your spiritual self or your inner self.

As I look at the world today, things are changing rapidly, and making sense of it all seems impossible. At times, it seems like we have entered into a madhouse. Everything we see and hear is wrapped up in fear, creating division and separateness, and at the same time we are more connected than ever before. We are led to believe we have no control and we are fearful of being controlled. The truth is, we do have total control. I wrote this book because I believe it is time we all wake up to who we are, and discover our own power to change our worlds for the greater good. My intent in writing this book is to share what I have discovered to be the most direct route to creating an empowered, magical, and desired life. It is also to awaken a sense of curiosity and an inner knowing of who we really are and our connection to the world we live in.

In my exploration, I always found myself asking, "Why does this work this way?" I had to go deep in my research to get to the "why" that resonated with me and helped me understand why I was able to create the things I desired in my life. I even questioned sharing this information in this book, which is Chapter 2, because I knew how uncomfortable it made me feel initially, and I wondered whether I really needed to challenge people's belief systems in such a deep way. However, I knew I needed to leave it in as it is the foundation on which everything else is built, and it is the true source of your hidden light. I will leave it up to you to decide if that rings true to you.

My desire is that you are able to use this book as a simple guidebook, which is filled with my personal examples, to discover your own abilities to create your positive and desired life experiences for yourself and the world around you. It is only through your own experiences that you will be able to discover your true power and your own truth.

~**Raana Zia**

Chapter One

Your Inner World Creates Your Outer World

"The greatest revolution of our generation is the discovery that human beings, by changing their inner attitudes of their minds, can change the outer aspects of their lives."

~William James
(American philosopher, 1842-1910)

Everything you experience is created by YOU. In other words, you create your own reality. Your external world is not separate from you, but it is directly connected to you. There is an energetic and spiritual force that connects everything in this Universe. And it is through this connected energy of all things seen and unseen that you create your reality. This powerful creative energy that emanates from inside of you, molds and shapes the Universe around you. More concisely, it is the energy of your thoughts, feelings, and beliefs that create all of your external experiences. This is not a theory or a concept; it is a Truth. This knowledge can be found in all religions and spiritual teachings if you dig deep enough. It has been hidden from you and has kept you from becoming your most authentic and liberated self. When you start to see the world in this new empowering way, you will see you have so much more power available to you than you may have previously thought. You will realize that you have the ability to be, do, or experience anything you desire, and the only real work you need to do is to learn HOW to align your inner thoughts, feelings, and beliefs CORRECTLY.

"We do not see things as they are. We see them as we are."
~Talmud

When you learn how to operate in a world that is energetically and spiritually connected to you versus separate from you, you will understand that all effort and energy must first be directed inward in order to most easily and directly achieve external experiences. This means that your thoughts, feelings, and beliefs need to first genuinely support the experience you desire before it can be created in your reality. Therefore, all conscious effort must first be directed towards creating and maintaining this internal alignment. By doing so, you will no longer waste your time pushing your energy outward, forcing things to happen, hoping things will happen, or straining and reaching for your goals. You will no longer react to situations, but instead, consciously create your situations by going inward. You will understand you have direct control over your day to day life if you choose. Things will happen easier for you and then anything will become possible. By learning how to operate from the inside first, you will unlock the key to living the life you were meant to live. You will learn who you really are.

Everything you think, feel, and believe creates all your experiences. Unfortunately, we have been led to believe it is the other way around. We have come to accept that everything we experience dictates how we think, what we feel, and what we believe. As a result, our experiences have shaped us into who we are and what we believe rather than the other way around. This inverted way of thinking and being makes us a slave to our past conditioning and current circumstances and strips us of our true powers to create. This way of thinking keeps us stuck in old patterns and makes it difficult for us to make any real change in our lives. By learning how to properly master your internal self, you will be able to tap into the highest part of yourself that has the power to change your reality to what you desire. You will realize you have the power to break out of old conditioned patterns simply by creating a new thought you truly believe in.

"What you think, you become. What you feel, you attract. What you imagine, you create."

~Buddha

In the past, I thought that working long hours accompanied by high levels of strain and stress in my corporate job would lead to success. I was conditioned to believe this based on my early experiences in the workplace. Many of my bosses expected their employees to work long hours as that showed dedication to the company and a commitment to delivering results. For years, I believed this point of view and I equated the numbers of hours worked to my level of commitment, performance, and productivity. I would average twelve-hour work days, and during busier periods I would work up to sixteen hours a day. I was recognized and appreciated for my efforts, which further reinforced my belief that I needed to keep working long and hard. For years, I even felt a sense of pride in what I was doing and how I worked, which again reinforced and supported my circumstances. Eventually, I realized my work life actually felt like work. I no longer enjoyed my workday.

I felt constantly stressed and was always thinking about my actions and how I was being perceived. I began living for the weekends and vacations to find relief. I realized I was spending 70 percent of my life working, and the majority of this time was full of frustration and unease. I was not happy and I needed my work life to change.

The birth of my first child was the catalyst for the change I desired. When I became a working mother, I had to balance my work life and home life. I decided I could no longer be stressed about work all the time or work around the clock. I believed I could still be a big contributor to the company and achieve my career aspirations while feeling a sense of joy, confidence, and ease at work. Once I got clear on this, and I believed it was possible, I began to relax internally. I refused to feel the old feelings of self-inflicted pressure about what others thought or expected from me. I consciously reduced my working hours from twelve hours a day to eight hours a day. I found I was far more productive and efficient in less working hours. Suddenly, I knew which tasks I needed to prioritize and which ones I didn't need to do. I let go of trying to do everything myself and trusted my team and other resources more. The work I was asked to do or expected to do, aligned with the time I wanted to put in. I suddenly felt a mastery of my position and a level of comfort that didn't exist before. My job became easier, yet I was able to accomplish more. Every day and week that passed, I felt more at ease and more joyful, and I was grateful for it. I loved this new way of being and I desired that it would continue. Believe it or not, my new reality at work was not because I was lucky or had special support or resources. Nothing external was the reason or cause for this change. The company did not change. In fact, my peers or colleagues continued to operate like they always did, by working long hours with a good amount of stress.

I realized that simply by creating a desire and aligning my beliefs and feelings to this desire, the world molded to me. When I relaxed, my world relaxed. Everything external to me supported my new internal being almost magically. In fact, my career accelerated even more rapidly than I had expected or hoped for. The higher I rose in my corporate career, the easier it was and the more fun I had, because I had established a new way of being. I always told people that I never worked at work, but the truth was, my work never felt like hard work again.

Most people do not realize that they can create the life they want in the way they want it. In fact, most people assimilate their lives to other people's lives, standards, or beliefs. They do not know how to use their internal energetic powers to shape their external reality. They do not know they can choose something different by making and committing to a different choice. You have more direct control over your life than you have been led to believe. You are an energetic being with incredible creative powers. Once you begin to understand that your world operates from the inside out, anything you desire becomes possible. The more you experience and are aware of your ability to create, the more powerful this ability will become.

"Do not conform to the pattern of this world, but be transformed by the renewing of your mind."
~Bible Romans 12:2

You Are Always Creating

You are always creating your reality whether you like what you are experiencing or not. All of your dominant thoughts, feelings, and beliefs are creating and impacting your reality in both positive and negative ways. Your positive conscious and directed thoughts, feelings, and beliefs are what allow you to successfully achieve a goal or attain what you desire. Your negative uncontrolled thoughts (mind chatter) or negative conditioned beliefs create unwanted experiences or prevent you from achieving your desires. When you want something and you are unable to achieve it, then your positive thoughts are impacted by negative thoughts, feelings or beliefs. Oftentimes, you do not realize that you are energetically negating your desires, but you are. Similarly, when things seem to work out for you with minimal effort, it is because internally you are in complete energetic alignment. This alignment of positive thoughts, feelings, and beliefs creates a powerful energetic force within you that connects with all that is unseen to bring into your physical reality that which you desire.

Think about a time when something worked out for you with very little effort. For example, you landed the right job, found the perfect apartment, met a great partner, got a really good deal on something, and so on. You might think things just worked out and you paid little attention to how and why. However, things happen for a reason. Deep down, you already know this. Your world is not random. The world you live in is intelligent and there is a logic and process by which everything happens. This intelligent process does not work outside of you. It is always directly connected to you and starts from you. This means you are directly responsible for all positive things that happen in your life, and you are responsible for all the negative experiences in your life. While it may be difficult to believe that you create your negative experiences, these are the experiences that teach you about what is within yourself and what thoughts, desires, or perspectives need to be changed. They can be your catalyst for self-discovery and growth if you see them for what they really are – your creation. When you learn how to consciously create a positive thought with an aligned feeling and belief, you can change any negative circumstance to the positive. The good news is that all thoughts, feelings, and beliefs can be changed, and only you have the power to change what is inside of you.

> *"As above, so below, as within, so without, as the universe, so the soul…"*
>
> ~**Hermes Trismegistus**

The Mirror Effect

Begin to see your external world as your mirror. Do not think of this as a metaphor, but a fact. See your reality as a reflection of your dominant thoughts, feelings, and beliefs. See the people you interact with and your circumstances as reflections of what is inside of you – what you believe about others and yourself. When you can look at your reality through this lens, you will start to see another layer of reality. You will begin to see that everything is you. Like a mirror, you will realize you cannot change your reflection by trying to change the mirror itself. Your reflection does not change until you change. The purpose of your mirror is to show you things as they are, and then you decide what, if anything, needs to change within you.

Sometimes your mirror becomes obvious to you (for example, when someone says something to you that is an exact reflection of what you were thinking in that moment), and other times it becomes less obvious unless you really pay attention. The first time I experienced and really understood that my reality was my mirror, I was contemplating a career change. I had been in the retail industry for sixteen years and I was no longer fulfilled. I knew I was not living my purpose. While I was not yet clear on my next step, I knew I needed a change. When I opened myself up to explore other job opportunities, I was immediately contacted by a recruiter for a chief financial officer position at another apparel retailer in the commutable area. I decided to explore this opportunity even though I was not thrilled that it was basically the same job but working at a different company. This job interview experience put me on a rollercoaster ride of emotional highs and lows that eventually forced me to acknowledge what was inside of me.

For a little background, I had become obsessed with finding my purpose in life a few years prior. During this time, I started a serious practice of mindfulness, and I developed a strong desire to contribute positively to the world in a way that was more than just making and selling clothes. I did not know how my new desires would translate into my next job, so when I got the call from the recruiter for this particular opportunity, I was open to learning more. Surprisingly, I discovered how unusual this company was and how directly aligned it was with my own personal values and desires. This company wanted to use business to do good in the world and they worked intensely towards this mission. They reflected my passion for purpose and took personal purpose seriously. I was even asked to come to one of my interviews ready to talk about my personal purpose; a subject that had been at the top of my mind for years. In addition, the company adopted the practice of mindfulness, and employees meditated for one minute before the start of most meetings. I found all of this highly unusual for an apparel retailer. I could not help but notice this particular opportunity was reflecting things back to me that I deeply valued and regularly thought about. I took this as a sign that this job might be right for me.

While my head rationalized why this could be perfect, my heart said something else. On the inside, I felt very unsure. After each interview, I felt glimmers of hope for something new, yet also a sense of discouragement that the change would not be big enough. The job itself was still a finance position similar to what I was currently doing. I kept wavering back and forth between thinking this opportunity was right for me and thinking it was wrong for me. The more confused I felt, the more baffling and overwhelming the process seemed to be. At one point, a friend asked me if I would take the job if I got the offer. Even though I was not feeling a sense of excitement or surety, I said I would accept it because it was meant to be. I did not believe I had the power to make my own decision, and I was driving myself crazy waiting for the "right" answer to be given. I could not understand why, on the one hand I was being presented with things I loved about this company, but on the other I was presented with the fact that this was everything I did not want. I finally realized the world was showing me exactly how I was feeling internally: confused! I was not yet clear on what I really wanted. Part of me wanted change, and the other part of me was willing for things to stay the same. It took four months for me to finally understand. I needed to make my own decision on whether I wanted the job or not. Deep down inside, I knew what I wanted and I needed to admit it to myself. Once I finally admitted that I did not want this job, I felt an overwhelming sense of relief. Two days later, I received the call that I did not get the job. Again, reality was reflecting my decision back to me. This experience was my wake-up call. I learned when I felt confusion internally, I got confusion in my experience; and when I finally had clarity, I got clarity.

When you start to see the world as your mirror, you will have a new sense of responsibility for your own life and you will feel empowered. Once I knew without a doubt that my reality is my reflection, I wielded the power to make bigger shifts for myself. I knew I could not create change if I did not have a clear thought or vision of what I desired. I was clear I wanted a career change, but frustrated because I did not know what that looked like or how change would happen. Internally, I felt clear that I no longer wanted to stay in my current position, and I did not want to work for another company doing what I was currently doing. I had decided that I needed four months off to figure out what I wanted to do next. However, leaving my job without having another job lined up was not a viable option because I needed the income to support my family. As time passed, my internal desire to leave the corporate world became stronger and stronger, and one morning I screamed to myself, "Get me out!" When my inner thoughts, feelings, and beliefs were finally aligned that I needed time off, my reality completely shifted. Two days after shouting "get me out!" I was laid off with twelve months of severance. While I wanted four months off, I got twelve months off fully paid. I was in awe. I knew I had created this experience, and I was hugely grateful to the universal forces that supported me. I was finally ready for a real change, and as a result, my reality shifted accordingly.

When you begin to internalize that everything outside of you is a reflection of what is inside of you, your reality becomes your feedback mechanism. Positive circumstances give you positive feedback, and negative circumstances tell you that something new needs to be created within you (a new perspective, thought, feeling, or belief). When you begin to recognize your own thoughts and beliefs in your external environment, you build much more self-awareness of your direct connection to your external reality. You no longer feel like a victim of your circumstances. When you are faced with an obstacle, challenge, break-up, or failure, your core being will know the circumstance is actually an opportunity, message, or catalyst for the positive change you desire if you consciously follow your inner guidance. There is much more power in knowing you create your reality, and there is less suffering, because nothing outside of yourself is to blame.

> *"He who controls others may be powerful, but he who has mastered himself is mightier still."*
>
> ~**Lao Tzu**

A New Discipline

To live your life from the inside out, you need to learn a new way of being. There is a knowledge, discipline, and practice required to effectively and consistently create your reality. Aligning your thoughts, feelings, and beliefs sounds simple to do, but we have lived our lives deeply conditioned into feeling, believing, and acting a certain way that any real change requires disciplined internal effort. For example, my unconscious thoughts and emotions when I lost my job would automatically go to the negative, even though I knew I had created the situation and this was the beginning of something better for me. There were times when these negative feelings would overwhelm me and I would be paralyzed with my deep conditioned fear of poverty. It took hard mental work to neutralize these thoughts of fear and keep them focused on my positive desires, but I knew I had to if I was committed to creating a positive change in my life. To create anything positive requires an aligned positive way of thinking and feeling. Negative thoughts and feelings only create negative situations. Managing your internal thoughts and emotions to the positive takes awareness and discipline.

Changing your life externally by first changing things internally will initially feel unnatural. Therefore, conscious creation is a discipline and a practice, until it becomes a more natural way of being, but it is well worth the internal effort. The purpose of this book is to awaken you to your own powers to create your reality, and provide you with a prescriptive method of practice. It is also meant to challenge you to see yourself and your world as much more than physical in nature, but also spiritual and energetic in nature. By learning how to tap into your spiritual and energetic resources, in addition to your physical resources, you can maximize your life experience. You can choose to experience love versus fear, joy versus sadness, abundance versus lack, or peace versus war. By understanding that the world works from the inside out, you will understand that each one of us has the power to change our worlds, and by doing so, we can change our collective world.

Your Inner World Creates Your Outer World

1. You are connected to everyone and everything by a creative energetic force.

2. You create your experiences through the energy of your thoughts, feelings, and beliefs.

3. You are always creating both your positive and negative experiences.

4. Your reality is your mirror. It is a reflection of what is inside of you. View your world this way and you will see the connected nature of your reality.

5. You can create any desired experience if you learn to manage and direct your internal energy correctly.

6. Operating from the inside out needs to become a practice and a discipline in order to overcome your conditioned tendencies, and most effectively create what you truly desire.

Chapter Two

Who You Are

"I cannot tell you any spiritual truth that deep within you don't know already. All I can do it remind you of what you have forgotten."

~**Eckhart Tolle**
(**spiritual author**)

The key to creating a life you truly desire lies in understanding who you really are and how your world works. Erroneously, we have been conditioned to believe that we are separate from everyone and everything in our reality, including the Ultimate Creator of the Universe. This viewpoint has stripped us of our true power to most easily and directly create the reality of our desire; and, as a result, we experience more struggle, stress, and frustration in our lives than is necessary. By waking up to who you are, and your spiritual nature, you will find you have access to all the resources you need to create the life you desire.

Many people think of materiality and spirituality as separate, distinct things. However, spirituality is, in fact, the creating principle of anything physical. Spirituality, as I refer to it, is not meant to be religious in context, but a belief in what is beyond the observable and physical realm. It is a belief in the Ultimate Creative force of the Universe. Within the spiritual realm there are energies and powers that exist, which are beyond what we see in the physical world. You have access to powers beyond the physical realm, and these powers lie within you because you are a spiritual being.

As you read this chapter, there may be things that do not resonate with you or that you initially reject because it feels uncomfortable, too out there, too esoteric, or too intangible. Even if you do not initially connect with the material, I encourage you to keep reading with an open mind. My intention is to present you with the "why" behind your creative abilities before sharing with you the "how." I want to set the context as to why you have the power to create and where your power ultimately comes from. This chapter is meant to push you to think beyond your physical world and open your thinking to your connection to something much greater. You do not need to believe what is stated in this chapter as a prerequisite to learning how to create your reality, which will be described in later chapters; however, I would not recommend skipping it completely.

You Are a Spiritual Being

You are not only your physical self. You are not only your body, mind, and personality (or what I will call your ego-self). Your true self is a part of you that is deep within you. It is your higher self, your soul-self, or your spiritual-self, and it is the part of you that is Divine. This is the part of you that is your Divine Light and which holds your greatest powers. Understanding who you really are is the biggest shift you will have to make in your thinking. This is the biggest secret that has been hidden from you.

Your physical ego-self is your mortal self. It sees itself as separate from everyone and everything. It lives in a world of fear, with the biggest being the fear of death. It is the part of you that holds you back from becoming who you are meant to be. You know this part of yourself because you have been identified with it all your life. You need no further explanation to help you understand. What you need to realize is that underneath the physical ego-self is your spiritual soul-self, your true self. This is the part of you that is immortal and directly connected to everyone and everything. This is the inner part of you that guides you. This is where all of your power is housed. It is time to reclaim this part of you and make it the dominant self in order for you to realize how powerful you truly are.

Your physical ego-self relies on the five senses to understand its experiences in the world. Everything you can see, hear, smell, taste, and touch is what is real to you. Your car, apartment, significant other, dog, and so on, are all real to you because you are able to physically interact with them. Your spiritual-self communicates to you through the sixth sense or your extra sensory perception. Your sixth sense is not physically observable. It is your intuition, your inner desires, your gut feelings, and your inner knowing. For example, have you ever had an inner drive or calling pulling you to do something? Have you ever had a gut instinct or an intuitive feeling about something that told you what to do or not do? I am sure you have because everyone has a sixth sense. This sense provides communication from your higher self, your spiritual-self, your connected self, and your true self. This unseen part of you is able to access information beyond your physical limitations. Your power lies in consciously connecting to this part of yourself and becoming fully aware that it exists.

Your sixth sense is a reminder that you are connected to something much bigger than yourself. Unfortunately, the material nature of the world we live in has taken us away from our spiritual selves. You may not experience your inner knowing or intuition as often as you would like because your intellect automatically rationalizes it away. You do not trust or believe in what your deepest self is telling you because you have become too dependent on believing through your five senses. You need to consciously make the hidden light in yourself stronger. You need to awaken your spiritual side and embrace the tools and resources it has given you to discover and create in this world.

"The Kingdom of God is Within You"

~Jesus LK 17:21

You Are Divine

Within you there is life energy that allows you to breathe, beats your heart, grows your bones, keeps your body and mind functioning, and many other amazing bodily tasks. This life force works through you and for you. You don't need to think about breathing – you just do it. This life force is also the life force of everything. It is in everything that has form (people, nature, all matter) and it is in the formless (empty space, silence). The life force that is within you and outside of you is the fabric of the Universe, the connective tissue. It is created by and is a part of the omnipresent and omnipotent force of the Universe that is called the Ultimate Creator, Source Energy, the Universe, God, or as I will refer to it – Cosmic Consciousness (the consciousness of the Universe in which the potential for everything exists). This means that the ultimate creative energy of Cosmic Consciousness is within you. You are not separated from Cosmic Consciousness, but you are one with it. To help you visualize what I mean, think of yourself as a wave in the ocean. As a single wave, you are distinct but completely connected to the greater ocean. This connected part of you is the spiritual part of you. You are one aspect of Cosmic Consciousness and, therefore, your true self is Divine in nature. Try not to let the word Divine make you feel uncomfortable. Take a moment and let your mind open up to the idea that the force that made the Universe left an imprint on you. You contain a spark of light or creative energy that came from the core of all creation.

Cosmic Consciousness creates all things, is in all things, and holds all things. There is nowhere that it is not. It contains all power, knowledge, and wisdom. It is all there is, has been, and ever will be. By being made up of this consciousness, you *are* this consciousness. You have access to all the power, knowledge, and wisdom there is. In the channeled book *The Impersonal Life* written in 1917 by Joseph Benner, it states that we (humans) are the only organisms on Earth that were given the ability to be self-aware of who we truly are, and be conscious of our Divine powers. This means it is now time that you become self-aware of your connection to the consciousness of the Universe. You are connected to the great creative force of everything. You are one aspect of the Divine but you have direct access to all that is Divine. This is why everything you need is inside of you. You need to clear away all of the conditionings created and housed in your physical ego-self in order to access this powerful part of you. From this place, you can create anything.

"All souls are immortal, but the souls of the righteous are immortal and divine"

~**Socrates**
(**Greek philosopher, 470-399 BC**)

You Are Immortal

The Divine part of you is immortal. Cosmic Consciousness is eternal, forever creating and expressing. In this lifetime, you are here to create and express an aspect of Cosmic Consciousness. Only you, deep down, know what your true purpose is. Similarly, everyone else you know is here to create and express an aspect of Cosmic Consciousness. We are all distinct yet we are all one. Cosmic Consciousness is infinite, so therefore there are infinite expressions of itself. Your current life experience in your physical body is but one expression of your infinite nature. When your body dies, your Divine self or soul will continue to exist. Then you will have another experience in which you will express another aspect of Cosmic Consciousness, and then another, and another, for eternity. Your soul is here to fully express itself and ultimately to know itself. Your soul uses your body to interact and experience the physical world, and uses your mind to create in the physical world. Your ego-self uses your body and mind in the same way. However, your ego-self creates limits on your experiences because it has limited knowledge, while your soul-self or spiritual-self is unlimited.

Your soul-self is eternal and, therefore, has no fear. There is no fear of death because there is no death for the soul. All your fear is in your ego-self. Your ego can and will die. Your ego wants to live and it will fight hard to stay the dominant part of you. So far it has been winning. Everything you fear comes from your ego-self. Everything that holds you back and puts up barriers comes from your ego-self. Everything that causes you suffering and pain comes from your ego-self. Your ego-self has been running your life while the most powerful part of you has been suppressed. Remember, all your power, wisdom, knowledge, and courage is in your spiritual or soul-self. It has the unlimited power to create anything because it is unlimited and has access to everything.

"The Universe is not outside of you. Look inside yourself; everything that you want, you already are."

~Rumi
(Sufi poet, 1207-1273)

You Are Connected to Everything

The connected nature of Cosmic Consciousness is important to understand. Behind and beyond everything is this fantastic energy force. We are taught in schools, through science, how we are connected to nature. For example, the trees give us oxygen to breathe, the sun provides energy for the trees to grow, life on earth needs water to survive, and so on. Therefore, we already know everything needs to work together in the natural world in order to create balance. At the spiritual level, our connectedness goes to a deeper level, the level of conscious energy or Cosmic Consciousness. Unfortunately, this deeper connectedness is not taught in schools. By knowing this level of connectedness, you can radically change your world for the better. Our true and deepest self is one with everything. Cosmic Consciousness is the Universe; therefore, the Universe is within you. Everyone and everything you experience within this physical world is within you. This means that I am you and you are me. You reflect a part of me, and I reflect a part of you. We are connected like a wave is to an ocean. Therefore, if I hurt you then I am hurting myself. If I give to you, I give to myself. Our innermost feelings reflect this relationship. This is why you feel good when you do good for others, or why you feel negative emotions when you harm someone. At the soul level, we can understand this, but at the ego level we do not.

There are moments in life that we all experience our cosmic connection. Most of the time we do not give much thought to these incidents and think of them as coincidence. For example, have you ever thought of someone who you haven't seen or talked to in a while and then, a short time later, that person either calls or texts you? Similarly, have you ever experienced a time when your friend says the exact thing you were thinking in the moment? That was not a coincidence, it was a connection. Your thoughts get directed to that person, and because of our connection through Cosmic Consciousness, the other person receives the signal and connects with you unknowingly.

In the book *Think and Grow Rich* written in 1937, the author, Napoleon Hill talks about the common philosophy that over five hundred men of great wealth used to create their success. Napoleon Hill met with and studied the most successful people of his time, including Andrew Carnegie, Theodore Roosevelt, Thomas Edison, John D. Rockefeller, Henry Ford, and Alexander Graham Bell. Through his research, he created a compilation of thirteen success principles, the final of which was the use of the sixth sense, or *The Door to the Temple of Wisdom*. This is the ability to tap into Infinite Intelligence in which all information and knowledge is stored, or in other words, the Cosmic Consciousness. The sixth sense can also be described as the connection between the finite mind and the infinite mind. This is where problems are solved and where creative inspiration or hunches comes from. This is where you get the warnings not to do something or the flashes of an idea to take action and do something. Everyone has access to this intelligence from within themselves because everything is within you. The more you go inside yourself through meditation and consciously tap into the connected part of you, the more you will find that you have access to all you need. Your experiences alone will show you your own powers.

You Are a Creator

Cosmic Consciousness is creation and it is always creating. You, as an attribute of Cosmic Consciousness, are also a creator and you are always creating. Yes, you are a Creator. Your purpose and nature is to create and express. It is your Divine power to create. The tool by which you create is your ability to think. Thinking is creating. Your thoughts create the world you experience in form (your inner world creates your outer world). Thoughts that enter into your mind have the Divine power to create. You are always creating your experiences based on your thoughts, whether you like them or not. Thoughts are energy forms that work through the connected nature of Cosmic Consciousness and manifest into form. Thinking is your power. Take a moment to truly understand that thinking is your most powerful and magical gift. Ask yourself, have you been using your Divine gift wisely, effectively, and optimally? If there is something you are currently dissatisfied with in your life, then the answer is no. However, do not judge yourself for answering no. We were never taught how to think. We were never taught the power of our thoughts. Without this self-awareness, our power has been suppressed. It is through the correct and disciplined use of your thoughts that you can create an experience of your desire with and through Cosmic Consciousness.

"Your thoughts create reality. The most pragmatic way to

create world peace is to use your power of visualization.
Think peace, act peace, spread peace, and imagine peace.
Your thoughts will soon cover the planet. The most
important thing is to believe in your power. It works."

~Yoko Ono
(multimedia artist)

You Can Change the World

One of the most harmful and false beliefs in our world today is that we have finite resources. How can this be when the very nature of Cosmic Consciousness is abundance? Cosmic Consciousness is infinite and always creating through itself. Therefore, there is no lack in the Universe. Lack is only experienced in the finite or from the ego-mind. Lack is a limitation and there is no limitation. Access your soul or spiritual mind and your reality becomes abundant. You can access anything or create anything. Your soul knows no fear and your soul knows life is abundant. Your soul is waiting for you to realize what it already knows, so you can experience what you came here to experience.

The world is currently working through the ego-minds of everyone with the belief that we are all separate: races, religions, countries, nations, and classes. We believe we are separate from God and nature. Our separatism mentality has created fear, conflict, wars, sadness, loneliness, and depression. This mentality assumes limits and that there is not enough for everyone. It promotes competition versus cooperation and harmony. We see others as either better than us or less than us. It does not make any sense, and as a result, it is hard to make sense of this world. What if we finally realized we are all connected, and we are all Divine beings who are but one aspect of the Ultimate Creator? How would the world change? Everything would naturally become the opposite. Fear would become love, because there would be nothing to fear. Our spiritual-selves know no fear. Without fear, conflict and wars would change to peace. Sadness, loneliness, and depression would move to joy, beauty, and happiness. This is possible. It is who we are and is our truest Divine nature. The only action to take is to wake up to your true self and learn how to use your Divine powers correctly. Become the person you are meant to be, so you can create the world you are meant to experience.

Who You Are

1. Spirituality and materiality are not separate and distinct things – the spiritual realm creates the physical realm.

2. You are both a physical and a spiritual being, and as a result you have both physical and spiritual resources you can access in order to fully experience the life you are meant to live.

3. You sixth sense or gut feelings, intuition, or inner knowledge is a reminder that you are more than just your physical self. You are part of something much bigger and you have access to knowledge beyond the logical and rational mind.

4. You were created by a Divine power, which has left within you your Divine spark; therefore, you are a Divine being with access to all that is Divine (all knowledge, wisdom, and power).

5. You are connected to everyone and everything through the same creative energy that created you – Cosmic Consciousness.

6. The coincidences you experience are really cosmic connections exemplifying the connected nature of the Universe.

7. You are an aspect of Cosmic Consciousness and your purpose and nature is to create and express. You are a creator, and through your thoughts you create your world.

8. When we finally realize that we are all connected and we are all Divine beings who are aspects of Cosmic Consciousness, our world will change for the greater good.

Chapter Three

How to Think

"Reality is built out of thought, and our every thought begins to create reality."

~Edgar Cayce
(American mystic, 1877-1945)

When the book *The Secret* by Rhonda Byrne came out in 2006, it introduced the concept of the Law of Attraction to millions of people worldwide, which addressed the power of positive thinking and how changing our thoughts can change our lives. *The Secret* was the first book I read on this concept. Something felt very true to me about the concept that our thoughts create, and I wanted to believe it could be that simple. However, I found it was not that simple. As a result, I started to conduct some deep research, as I was determined to understand how the world worked and how I could create what I wanted in my life. I discovered that the key is correct thought, and we were never taught how to think correctly. Thinking is a power we were all given in order to create in this world. Growing up, I had never seen thinking as a Divine creative power and, as a result, I did not know when I was fully utilizing my powers and when I was misusing them. In our connected Universe, our thoughts are the way in which we direct the universal energetic powers to bring our desires into physical form. Our thoughts create in our reality through their own spiritual energy. When you understand

and practice correct thinking, you will see you have the power to create anything you truly desire. And then you will experience life differently.

Most people think they already know how to think because thinking is something we do automatically. However, by thinking everything in this world is separate from you and outside of you, you have been thinking incorrectly. By being unconscious that your thoughts create, you have been thinking incorrectly. If you are struggling to achieve something, then you are thinking incorrectly. When you feel fear and anxiety, you are thinking incorrectly. I am sure there are times when you do think correctly and you achieve what you set out to accomplish, but did you know at that time you were thinking correctly? Did you know what you were doing? If you knew what you were doing you would probably be doing it more often. In order to most efficiently and easily create your desires, a mastery of thinking is required. If you master your thinking you will become the master of your life, but to master anything it takes knowledge, discipline, and practice. This chapter is meant to give a high-level overview on what it means to think correctly. In later chapters, I will go into more detail about how to create most effectively.

Unconscious Thoughts

When I say that you are not thinking correctly, I mean you are not always consciously thinking and controlling your thoughts. Any thought that is not a controlled, purposeful, and supportive thought, I refer to as an unconscious thought. Unconscious thinking is when your mind is thinking on its own by pulling in thoughts based on past experiences, programmed fears, other people's ideas, and things buried in your subconscious from your past conditioning. These thoughts are the voices that are constantly talking in your head, filling any void in your mind space. They are always running in the background as mind chatter unless you consciously stop them. Unconscious thinking is not productive thinking. These are the thoughts that cause you to automatically or uncontrollably react to things. These are the thoughts that fill you with unease, fear, anxiety, or stress. These are the thoughts that keep you stuck in old patterns or habits.

It is important to understand what unconscious thoughts are because much of this thinking is wasted energy or thoughts that hold you back from expressing your true potential and your true self. The most dangerous unconscious thoughts are those which are negative in nature. These include negative thoughts about yourself (*I am not smart enough, I am not capable, I am not lovable, I am not lucky*, etc.), your imagined negative thoughts about yourself from others (*he doesn't like me, she thinks I am inferior, he thinks I am not capable, she thinks I am not a risk taker*, etc.), invented negative future circumstances (*I will be hurt, I will fail, I will lose all my money, she/he will leave me*, etc.), past negative circumstances (*my heart was broken, I failed before, I come from poverty, I was treated poorly*, etc.), thoughts about other people (*she is such a horrible leader, he is not a good friend, she is not as smart as I am, I am jealous of him*, etc.). These thoughts are automatic and hold you back from creating something positive because they are negative. Negative thoughts create negative experiences. If you continue to let these thoughts automatically run in the background, you are not using the power of your thinking to your benefit and you will continue to create undesirable experiences.

"Thoughts become things. If you see it in your mind, you will hold it in your hand."

~Bob Proctor
(speaker, author, coach)

When I made the jump to chief financial officer in my career, it validated my ability to manifest my desires. My positive thoughts of what I desired to do and be, and where I desired to live manifested in my life sooner and easier than I had expected. In this new position, I found myself in the perfect situation of loving what I did and loving the people I worked with. Interestingly enough, I found myself constantly thinking about how awful my prior boss was and how frustrated and angry he made me feel. When these thoughts and feelings from my past came into my head, I told myself they were helping me appreciate how great my current job was, and I allowed these thoughts to continue racing through my mind. However, I later found out these thoughts were not helping me. A couple months into my new job, all those feelings from my past came into my present. I found myself in a very challenging relationship with a peer at work. This person was someone who I had to work with and build credibility with in order to be successful in my new position. He was someone I got along with when I first joined, but suddenly everything changed and I could not understand why. It became an intense situation where I was made to feel inferior, and he made several attempts to discredit me. The feelings of anger and frustration felt very familiar to the feelings I had towards my former boss. I had to constantly manage and deal with the negative energy being directed towards me. At first, I could not believe this was happening, and then it hit me that I had created this with my thinking. I knew

I did this. My unconscious negative thoughts about my past had created this situation in my present. Not only was I capable of consciously creating good things in my life, I was capable of unconsciously creating negative things. All thoughts have the power to create, so be mindful of what thoughts dominate your mind space.

> *"It is the mark of an educated mind to be able to entertain a thought without accepting it."*
>
> ~**Aristotle**
> (**Greek philosopher, 384-322 BC**)

Other people's thoughts have the power to automatically shape how you think, what you say, how you act, and what you create. These thoughts, if they are negative and/or unsupportive to your desires, are unconscious thoughts. They can be thoughts from your parents based on their belief system, thoughts based on what you are told from the media, thoughts based on your religious institutions, society, cultural upbringing, and so on. Examples of these type of thoughts include: *there is much to fear in this world* (from the media), *money is the root of all evil* (from religion), *boys are smarter than girls* (from culture or society), *life is a struggle* (from family), and so on. These are thoughts that have come from outside yourself and they have the potential to be either knowingly or unknowingly accepted as true. For example, I grew up in a culture that believed that in order to be successful in life you needed to become a doctor, lawyer, or engineer. I grew up in a religion that saw men as superior to women. I grew up and lived in a country where being stressed is normal. I now choose not to believe any of these things. You need to find the beliefs that support you and which are true for you. The key to understanding what thoughts and beliefs are supportive to you is to question why you think the way you do about something. Ask yourself: Is this what I really believe or did this come from someone else? Are these thoughts true? Are these thoughts positive or negative? Do these thoughts support me?

By distinguishing between your true thought versus someone else's thought, you will make both big and little shifts in your life. I grew up in a family that believed it is irresponsible to spend a lot of money on vacations. I rejected this belief, and since then I have been experiencing luxury vacations in beautiful places. I rejected a cultural thought that men are the providers of the family, which has allowed me to successfully grow my own career and provide for my family. I rejected the thought I was not a pet person because I came from a family that did not have pets, and now we have an adorable dog loved by all my family. Assess your own thoughts. Question deeply why you think the way you do. Decide for yourself what thoughts you want to hold on to, and what thoughts support the life you want to create. If your thoughts are negative and/or do not support who you are and what you desire, then they are unconscious thoughts.

"Until you make the unconscious conscious, it will direct your life and you will call it fate."

~C.G. Jung
(Swiss psychiatrist, 1875-1961)

Conscious Thinking

Your real power to create what you desire is through your conscious thinking. Conscious thinking is thinking that is purposeful, positive, and directed by you. These thoughts are your intentions, desires, goals, and ambitions. More importantly, conscious thoughts are aligned with your heart and have the added power of belief and positive emotion in them. They are whole and confident thoughts and they must be aligned with belief and positive emotion or else they will not manifest.

Many times, we think we are consciously thinking, but we are not because our thought is not yet aligned with our beliefs and emotions. This usually happens when we are looking for a change which is different from what we have experienced before. You may say you want an abundance of money, a successful career, a new relationship, a life of happiness, a peaceful society, and so forth, but do you fully believe that something new is possible? Do you believe it in your heart? If your desires are not manifesting then your inner thoughts, feelings, and emotions are out of alignment. There are unconscious or negative thoughts blocking your positive desires. The biggest barriers to your desires are fear and doubt. You need to really assess the beliefs and emotions you have around your desires. You cannot doubt your ability to create. Conscious thoughts need to be confident with a faith that the spiritual forces of Cosmic Consciousness are working on your behalf. Know that you have the ability to change any belief and emotion to your benefit. If you want something new, do not let your past experiences control your beliefs. Instead, believe in who you really are – a powerful and Divine creator of your reality.

A complete conscious thought will consciously create your desires. I have a friend who once told me she wanted to live somewhere warm. She pictured herself in a place with palm trees. At the time, she did not know how it would happen, but she knew it would. A few years later she met her husband and moved from New York to Los Angeles. Similarly, I met a woman who consciously decided she wanted to leave her marketing job and start her own interior decorating firm. She saw it, felt it, and believed it because she understood the power of conscious thinking. She is now several years into her successful new business. Conscious thoughts apply to any aspect of your everyday life, whether you desire a table in a popular restaurant, tickets to a sold-out Broadway show, a prime parking spot, or a productive and fulfilling day. The key is to know you have the power to create your desires by the spiritual energy of your intentions and your faith in the creative process.

"You have power over your mind, not outside events. Realize this, and you will find strength."

~**Marcus Aurelius**
(Roman Emperor, 121-180 AD)

Building Awareness and Control

It is important that you understand the difference between unconscious thoughts and conscious thoughts for yourself by becoming fully aware of your thoughts. Having awareness of your own thoughts and having the ability to control your thoughts are necessary in order to consciously create your reality effectively. Spend time getting to know yourself and your thought patterns. Remember, all your thoughts are powerful. All your thoughts are creative. Your dominant thoughts are your most powerful thoughts and they will create whether you want them to or not.

I practiced being consciously aware of my thoughts on my drive to and from work, around twenty minutes each way. I kept the radio turned off and focused my attention on driving and being present, with the intention of consciously not thinking about anything else. Every once in a while, I would lose my focus, and thoughts would enter my head. I would catch myself and observe my thoughts, wondering why these specific thoughts showed up. I would then ask myself, *are these thoughts helping me now?* The answer was always no, and I would consciously focus on driving again. It is a very interesting process when you start to observe your unconscious thoughts. You quickly learn how random and useless they are.

You can start to bring awareness to your thoughts at any time of the day. When you are working out, eating breakfast, or doing any task that does not require your full brainpower. You can even sit quietly with your eyes closed and put focused attention on your thoughts. Ask yourself: What am I thinking right now? Why am I thinking these thoughts? Are these thoughts helping me? Are these thoughts positive or negative? Are these thoughts mine? The purpose of this exercise is for you to become aware of what is in your mind. Try to do this as often as you can. The more frequently you do this, the more often you will notice how much of your mind space is filled with unconscious thinking.

> *"Rule your mind or it will rule you."*
> ~**Horace (Roman poet 65-8 BC)**

One of the most powerful skills you can have is the ability to stop thinking. By being able to stop all thoughts at any time of the day, you become the master of your thoughts. You become in control of your thoughts rather than your thoughts controlling you. When you are in control of your thoughts, you control the creation of your reality. One highly effective way to build the ability to control your thoughts is through meditation. Meditation is a practice that helps you cease all thinking and connects you to a space beyond all thought. When you meditate, you clear your mind, relax your body, and become fully alert. When you initially start the practice, clearing your mind from all thoughts can be a challenge, as thoughts flow in automatically. Through conscious effort and practice, you will soon become more adept to stopping your thoughts at any time you choose. There are many different techniques for learning how to meditate, so find the one that works for you. Meditation is a highly-recommended practice because it disciplines your mind and is a way in which you can access your Divine connected self.

When you can effectively stop your thoughts, your body will feel more at ease. The more you are in this state of ease and freedom from thought, the more powerful you will become. Your energy becomes centered within you and builds a greater force because it is not wasted on unconscious thinking or uncomfortable feelings. As a result, when you consciously think something, there is more energy available for your conscious thought to create. You build your creative power by your ability to control your mind.

I don't like mind chatter and unconscious thinking. All of the thoughts that swirl around in my head create unease, problems to solve, and they are an unproductive use of my mental energy. Once I saw how much easier things became when I consciously stopped thinking, I realized how much I loved not thinking. This may seem counter-intuitive since we have been conditioned to believe that thinking is a good thing. However, not all thinking is good for you.

If all thoughts are creative, then you should only use your mental energy to think thoughts that serve you.

When you build the muscle to stop thinking, then you have the foundation you need to reprogram how you think in a way that serves you and is focused correctly. Correct thoughts are those which focus only on what you desire, and not on the opposite. This means, if you are focused on creating a new future, stop thinking about the past. Even if the past is filled with good memories, you are still holding onto the past and you will be unable to move forward into your desired future. This is easier said than done and it takes a lot of mental commitment to stop thinking about the past. If you are looking for a new relationship, you have to stop thinking about your old relationship. This almost seems impossible to some people, but once you are able to master it, you will find a new relationship will appear. New experiences appear when you allow them to, by letting go of thoughts or attachments to old experiences. This can take time and effort, but the more you can control your thoughts, the quicker you will be able to make a change.

"The energy of the mind is the essence of life."
~**Aristotle (Greek philosopher, 384-322 BC)**

Thoughts Are Energy

Everything that is seen and unseen is made up of the energy of Cosmic Consciousness. Everything physical and non-physical is made up of the same connected creative energy. The Universe is an energetic vibrational field. Solid matter, such as a chair or a table is energy vibrating at a slow and dense rate. Thoughts which are unseen are energy vibrating at a higher vibrational rate. There isn't anything that is not part of this creative energetic field, and the only differentiating factor is the frequency or rate of vibration. Science, through quantum physics, is proving what spirituality has known to be true – that everything is connected and comes from the same source of energy.

Your thoughts create because they are a spiritual energetic force that communicates with the energetic field of Cosmic Consciousness. The Universe responds to the vibration of your thoughts by bringing together into physical form that which matches the vibration of your thoughts. The language of the Universe is energetic vibration. We have the Divine ability to communicate with the universal forces by managing our vibration through our thoughts. Thoughts are our energy and energy is power. Therefore, you need to be conscious of what you think and where you direct your creative energy and power.

Negative thoughts equate to negative energy. If you put your energy into negative thoughts you give those thoughts more energy and more power to create. For example, think about a time when you were angry at someone. Did you find yourself focused on the situation that made you angry for an extended period of time? Did you continue thinking about more situations with that person that made you angry? Did that then make you get angrier and angrier? The reason why your anger persists is because you continue to feed more energy to the feeling of anger through your thoughts. I have been in this state many times before and it never leads to anything good. It is only when I stop giving energy to these negative thoughts that the negative experience stops. You can choose where you direct your energy, so choose wisely.

Always put your thought energy towards the positive and not the negative. Direct your energy towards the solution and not the problem, or to the goal and not the barriers.

The next time you are faced with a situation that appears to be negative, stop thinking into the negative aspect of the situation and giving it energy. Remember, your energy has creative power. For example, I used to get all worked up at my job if someone made a significant mistake. After all, I managed the numbers and people relied on my team for accurate information. I felt highly accountable for presenting accurate information, and if information presented was wrong, this would create a great deal of anxiety for me because I felt it was a direct reflection on my credibility. For years, when mistakes were found, I would project outwards and cause other people on my team to feel my stress. I would think into the problem more than I needed to and I would spend un-necessary energy worrying about the consequences. As a result, I would micromanage solutions and drive myself and my team crazy. I would feel stress and anxiety with the feelings of fear motivating me to problem solve. I became conditioned to respond in this manner, and I believed my high work standards justified it. While this reaction worked in the past to eventually find a solution, it always created unease and stress along the way for myself and others. When I finally discovered that my thinking, feelings, and beliefs create my reality, I decided to take a new inward approach to the next big problem that came up at work. I wanted to prove to myself that I could create the reality I wanted by changing how I thought and felt internally. I decided I would not put any thought into my fears (fear of what would happen due to this mistake). I consciously stopped my negative thinking and feelings of stress. I relaxed my mind and body and trusted that a solution would come to me the next day. The following day, like magic, all aspects of the problem were gone. The team did their due diligence, fixed the issues, spoke with all involved parties, and everything became a non-issue. I avoided creating unnecessary stress on myself and unwanted pressure and stress on my team. I clearly saw for myself the power of stopping the runaway negative thinking, and the importance of not putting energy into a negative projected outcome. Since then, I have always gone inward first to align my energy correctly, proving time and time again that all my power is within. The source of energy is inside of you and, as a result, you need to go within to align your energy with what you desire.

"Where the mind goes energy flows."
~Earnest Holmes
(American New Thought author, 1887-1960)

When you no longer give energy to negative thoughts or unconscious thinking, you are conserving your energy for the positive things you desire in your life. This is similar to conserving the energy in your physical body. You might decide not to go hiking all day if you know you have plans to go dancing at night. Similarly, you know if you get a good night's sleep before a big race the next day, you will run a lot better and quicker than if your body is tired. You want to have the optimal amount of energy to maximize your experience. By conserving your thoughts, you maximize the power of the thoughts you choose to think. Therefore, you should think only when you need to. Avoid making up scenarios in your head to create unnecessary thinking. Conserve your energy for when you really need it. The trap we fall into is that we are automatically creating made-up things to think about. We are constantly thinking about things in our past, or things in the future. The most direct way to conserve our thought energy is to stay in the present.

Always remember not to give your energy away to anyone else. Do not let someone else think for you. This is extremely important. Sometimes it is easier to give your power to someone else. Many times, you do not even realize you are doing this. This is because you do not yet fully understand who you truly are and the Divine powers you have. There is nothing outside of yourself that can create your experiences unless you allow it to by your thoughts and beliefs. For example, I asked a friend how it was going with her relationship. She didn't seem truly happy with her circumstance. She was dating someone who was married and a decision needed to be made regarding whether or not they were going to be together. I knew she wanted to be in a committed relationship. Deep down, she knew what she wanted, but she opted to let him decide her future. She was okay with waiting for him to decide. This happens all the time because we do not realize we have given our power away to someone else. When you give your power away, you become powerless and your energy gets drained. Instead, your thoughts need to be directed inward. This is when you need to decide what you really want. You need to reframe your thinking to serve and empower yourself. Thinking is your Divine power. Use your ability to think wisely and purposely, and do not give your power away.

How to Think

1. Unconscious thinking is incorrect thinking – these are thoughts that are uncontrolled and can be harmful if you are not aware of them and if you let them persist.

2. Conscious thinking is correct thinking. Conscious thoughts are thoughts that have the added power of feeling and belief.

3. Start to become aware of your thoughts and your own thought patterns. Be able to distinguish for yourself between a conscious thought and an unconscious thought.

4. Learn how to stop thinking – this is a muscle you need to build to stop unconscious and harmful thoughts from blocking the creative power of your conscious positive thoughts.

5. Know that your thoughts are spiritual creative energy. Conserve your mental energy and only use your thoughts to consciously create.

6. Do not give away your Divine power to create to someone else.

Chapter Four

The Use of Speech

"Language creates reality. Words have power. Speak always to create joy."

~Deepak Chopra
(New Thought author)

Many people associate speech as a tool for communication with others. While this is true, it is also a communication tool with the creative energy of the Universe. This means that your words communicate to both what is seen in this physical reality (your friends, family, co-workers, strangers) and to what is unseen (Cosmic Consciousness) in the spiritual world at the same time. As a result, words have much more power than you realize. If you learn how to speak correctly and harness the power and energy of the unseen, then your words will become a powerful tool in creating your desired reality.

Words, like thoughts, are energy, have a vibration, and are creative. Your spoken words are sounds that reflect your thoughts. Sound, vibration, and energy make up the entire Universe. You are connected to your Universe through this energy; so therefore, what you put out in words impacts you directly. When the energetic vibration of your thoughts and words are positively aligned, you generate a greater creative force that has the ability to accelerate the manifestation of your desire in your physical world. The energy projected by spoken words can be disruptive and can be the catalyst for the change you desire. Your ability to speak is a Divine ability and should be used thoughtfully. In other words, think before you speak.

In our physical world, most people understand that words have power. We know if we say something hurtful to someone, we can cause them pain. We also know if we compliment someone, we can make them feel good. We can use our words to manipulate people into doing what we want. We can use our words to create beautiful poetry that uplifts and inspires. In our world today, politicians are very careful about the words they speak in order to create support and acceptance amongst the voting public. Lawyers are very careful with the words they choose in order to defend or protect their clients. Doctors are very careful with the words they use with their patients so as not to put themselves at risk of liability. Marketers know the power of words in creating campaigns or company mission statements. Sales people have a strategy with words, which includes knowing when to speak and not to speak in order to close the deal. Children know the power their words have to make their parents or teachers happy. The power our words have on influencing and impacting others is easy to understand since we see this in action everywhere. While you know the impact your words have on other people, are you aware of the impact your words have on you? Did you know your words have the power to create your reality?

"The words you speak become the house you live in."

~**Hafiz**
(**Sufi poet, 1326-1389**)

Speak What You Want, Not What You Don't Want

Words are energetic vibrations that represent a thought, and your thoughts create. Words spoken with confidence, conviction, and belief have the power to remove energetic barriers and bring about your conscious desires. This means, you can give your desired thought strength to create if you speak your desire out loud. If you keep it inside, you might be holding it back. Speak your positive desire with confidence, even if it scares you or even if you don't know how it will happen. Saying what you desire out loud, even if it is to yourself, is more beneficial than keeping it inside. For example, if you want to open your own yoga studio in Bali, say it out loud, even if you don't know how it will happen. If you want to write and play music for a living, say it out loud. If you want to make a successful presentation in front of the entire company, say it out loud. Say it with confidence and conviction. Say it with heart and feeling. Use your words to create the clarity to the Universe. Speaking your desire is like the start gun at the beginning of a race. Your words mean GO.

In the creative process, speech needs to be used literally and directly. The words that are spoken need to clearly and positively align with your desires. The key is the word positive. Say what you want and not what you don't want. It is that simple. By saying what you don't want, you give energy to what you don't want. This energy is negative and counteracts what you truly do want. If both your thoughts and words are directed to what you don't want, you will create what you don't want. Take a moment to read that again. Never say what you don't want. While it is beneficial to know what you don't want, don't put any energy into it. It is more important for you to get clear on what you do want. Both your thought energy and speech energy should always be directed toward what you want. If you want to be in a relationship, do not say, "I don't want to be alone," but instead say, "I want to be in a relationship." If you are sick, don't say, "I don't want to be sick," but instead say, "I want to be healthy." If you say what you don't want using words like "alone" or "sick" this is what you will create with the energy of your thoughts and words. The words "relationship" and "healthy" are both positive and clear. The energetic and spiritual language of the Universe is precise and there is no room for interpretation, so you need to be clear and direct with what you say.

Listen to the words you use and know their power. You can always catch yourself when you say what you don't want, and immediately change it to what you do want. You can realign your words and thoughts to serve your greatest desires. Think about all the negative events shown on the news every day; all of the violence and conflict. Most people respond to what they are seeing and reading by saying what they don't want. "I don't want war," "I don't want violence," "I don't want terrorists coming into this country," "I don't want higher taxes," and so on. If we are collectively focusing on what we don't want, then we will never experience what we truly want.

It is easy to talk about problems because everyone has them. Sometimes problems are the common ground in which people have something to discuss with one another. We have all been in conversations where people were complaining about their boss, job, relationship, health, finances, the weather, the government, and so on. If your true desire is to make something better, then stop speaking into the problem and start speaking into the solution. You might find it is harder to do, but problems can only be solved when you focus on the solution. The more you talk about the problem, the more the problem persists. Change your thoughts and words towards what you desire and then you will experience your true spiritual power.

"We cannot solve our problems with the same thinking we used when we created them."

~Albert Einstein
(theoretical physicist, 1879-1955)

Words Build Belief

Words can also be used to help you build a belief in your desired thought. For example, affirmations are often used to build a positive belief about oneself. Affirmations can be defined as positive statements that you repeat to yourself proclaiming something you desire to be true. By saying this statement over and over again, with conviction, for an extended period of time, you are able to create a new belief. As a result, you can consciously use the power of words to help you change a deep-rooted belief that limits you from achieving what you truly desire, to a belief that supports you. Examples of positive affirmations are: "I am loved," "I am worthy," "money is abundant," "I am successful," "I am brave." When you first say an affirmation, you begin at a place of acknowledging you do not yet deeply hold this belief. The sincere and faithful repetition finally creates a new belief in the subconscious mind. When a new belief and thought is created, a new reality is then created. The energy and conviction of the words spoken have the power to plant and grow a new supportive belief. There has been much written about affirmations as a technique to create positive beliefs. Tony Robbins, in his documentary *I Am Not Your Guru* talks about how he would affirm to himself,

"I am unstoppable" when he was out running. He states that after saying it over and over, he could not help but believe it. If a thought about yourself is holding you back, know that your words can be a tool to change your beliefs about yourself, and decide if using affirmations is the right strategy for you.

I have heard people say if you say it enough times, then people will believe you. I have seen this to be true. In the corporate world, marketers use this strategy all the time to create a belief. Think about the slogan for Las Vegas – "what happens here, stays here." The slogan represents a made-up idea that you can go to Las Vegas and have the freedom to be and do what you can't do at home. It also represents the idea that whatever you do there will not follow you back to your normal daily life. The repetition of this slogan has created a general belief about the Las Vegas experience thus making it a very popular tourist destination. Similarly, slogans such as BMW's "The Ultimate Driving Machine," American Express' "Don't Leave Home Without It," Apple's "Think Different," and many more are developed to create a belief, which then influences people to buy. Our corporations know how to use the power of the word for their benefit, so why don't you use the power of words for your benefit? Create your own slogan that represents who you want to be and say it over and over again until you believe it. Once you believe it, you will be it.

"We have to retrain our thinking and speaking into positive patterns if we want to change our lives"

~Louise Hay
(New Thought author)

Keep your Words Positive

Keep your words positive to bring positive energy to yourself and your world. My nine-year-old daughter, Samar, seems to have always known this. She is a very wise soul and I look at her as my teacher. Her whole being radiates positive energy. Even in her toughest times, she finds a way to use positive thoughts, words, and actions to create her reality. Since Samar started going to school, she always enjoyed it. She loved her teachers and was always friendly with all the students in her class. Samar gave her teachers hugs and affection, and they always appreciated how sweet and caring she was. It was not until she reached the third grade that this all changed for her. She found herself with a teacher who didn't connect with her in the affectionate way she was used to. This made her feel dismissed and ignored. She also felt like she was always doing something wrong, which was hard for me – as her mother – to see. The teacher was loved by many parents because of her no-nonsense style; however, this was not the best fit for Samar. I looked at this experience as something that would make my daughter stronger. While it was tough on her, it was amazing how she navigated the situation. She told me every morning she would wake up and think she was going to have the best day ever. She would consciously think in order to create her day. She also told me she would say out loud to her teacher that she was the best teacher. Samar knew she was not the best teacher for her, but she told me she needed to say that to make herself feel good. I was amazed when she said that to me, as I knew exactly what she was doing. She was creating a positive belief about her teacher so she would not focus on the negative. She knew she could not have a good experience if she thought about things that were negative. She used her words to create a positive thought and experience.

Often, we are confronted with situations that hurt, disappoint, or anger us. These are the times when speaking positively can feel virtually impossible. While you should feel your emotions, and acknowledge what just happened, know that the more you think and speak into the negative situation, the more you feed it. You are giving it the energy of thoughts and words. By doing so, you are prolonging your misery and likely making it worse. You need to stop speaking into it before you can stop thinking into it. Once you stop thinking into it, you stop the negative creative process. Think of a time when someone hurt you or betrayed you in some way. Did you talk about the situation with your friends or family? How often did you talk about it? How did it feel when you talked about the situation or the person involved? Did this hurt you or help you? You might think it helped you because you were able to get all your anger out. Sometimes people have to spiral downwards before they reach the point where they can't take it anymore. Regardless, realize that nothing gets better or changes until you let go and stop speaking and thinking into the negative. The timing of when you want to move on to something better, or the degree to which you want to feel bad will determine when you decide to stop speaking and thinking into the negative.

You can dramatically change your world by consciously choosing to speak positively. You know the saying you were told as a child: "If you can't say something nice, then don't say anything at all." Intellectually, this makes sense if we want to live in a peaceful world. Spiritually, it means that if you speak positively you create positive energy for yourself and everything around you. Your positive words represent your positive thoughts. This creates an internal energy alignment in your body. When you are being positive in your inner world, your external world will reflect back positive experiences. Negative words, since they represent a negative thought, have a counter-effect on your positive thoughts, creating negative experiences. This is how the spiritual world works. If you want to create a change in anything, use all your power wisely. If there is nothing positive to say, then do not say anything at all. Keep your energy directed to the positive in everything you say. By doing so, you are making yourself a more powerful creator of your reality. Your goal should be to maximize your spiritual power to more easily create the world you desire. The goal is not perfection. Do not judge yourself if you say something negative or think something negative. The goal is to do that less often than you currently do now and experience the increased creative benefits it brings you.

"Before you speak, let your words pass through three gates. At the first gate, ask yourself, 'Is it true?' At the second gate ask, 'Is it necessary?' At the third gate ask 'Is it kind?'"

~**Rumi**
(**Sufi poet, 1207-1273**)

The Use of Speech

1. Your words communicate to both what is seen in this physical reality (your friends, family, co-workers, strangers, etc.) and to what is unseen (Cosmic Consciousness) in the spiritual world at the same time.

2. Words, like thoughts, are energy, have a vibration, and are creative. Your spoken words are sounds that reflect your thoughts.

3. You can give your desired thought energetic strength to create if you speak your desire out loud.

4. Speak what you want and not what you don't want. The energetic and spiritual language of the Universe is precise and there is no room for interpretation, so you need to be clear and directed in what you say.

5. Use your words to create supporting beliefs. The use of positive affirmations can help you build a new positive belief.

6. Keep your words positive to bring positive energy to yourself and your world.

Chapter Five

The Power of Feelings

"Emotions are what make us human. Make us real. The word 'emotion' stands for energy in motion. Be truthful about your emotions, and use your mind and your emotions in your favor, not against yourself."

~Robert Kiyosaki
(investor and author)

Emotions are life energy inside of you. Emotional energy is an extension of your thought energy. It is your body's response to a thought that you physically feel. This energy has the incredible power to create your desires if it is managed and directed appropriately. You need to think of emotions as creative energy that gets triggered by a thought. A negative emotion is triggered by a negative thought and a positive emotion is triggered by a positive thought. Your feelings and emotions are your compass for what is going on in your inner world. Therefore, they are an incredible gift and tool to help you understand if you are internally aligned with your positive desires. When you feel good or at ease in your body, you are embodying your most powerful creative self. Positive emotions will always lead to positive experiences. The challenge comes when we are faced with negative emotions. It becomes difficult to manage that energy and we typically keep feeding our negative thoughts and building more energy that blocks our positive desires. The key is to understand the power of our emotions, both positive and negative, and know that even your negative emotions can serve and support you if the energy is transformed and directed correctly.

Energetically, not all emotions are created equal. Some emotions are more powerful than others. On the negative spectrum of the emotional scale there is shame, guilt, fear, jealousy, anger, worry, and so on. On the positive side there is passion, optimism, happiness, joy, gratitude, and love. Negative emotions vibrate energetically at a low frequency while positive emotions vibrate at a high frequency. Why does this matter? The higher the frequency of the emotion, the easier it is to create what you desire. When you put yourself at a higher frequency of energetic vibration, you are more closely aligning yourself with the positive force that creates all things – Cosmic Consciousness. By staying in positive emotional states, you are awakening the spiritual part of you that has all the power to serve and support you. If you study spirituality and try to gain an understanding of this life force that is within and all around us, you will learn that the ultimate nature of Cosmic Consciousness is the frequency of love. Love is positive. Therefore, any emotion that is positive will bring you closer to the power of all creation. Similarly, as you move further from love, the further you are from the great creative force. The lower your vibrational state, the greater the barrier or resistance to creating anything you truly desire. The low vibration emotions do not serve you and keep you stuck in old patterns unless you know how to transform them and redirect the energy. These negative emotions can keep you trapped in your own prison. When you stay stuck in a low vibration you are no longer in control of your reality. Instead, you are controlled by what is external to you.

In our world today, it is easy to feel negative emotions such as fear, worry, jealousy, frustration, and anger. We feel these feelings all the time, and half the time we don't even know we are feeling them. We have become conditioned to live in this negative emotional state as our baseline state and think this is normal. When was the last time you turned on the news and felt good about the world? When was the last time you saw an advertisement or looked at a magazine and felt good about yourself? It seems like our external environment is doing all it can to keep us in a low vibrational state, and away from the higher frequencies that are connected to our powerful soul selves. This is why it has become easy to feel and stay in negative emotional states. Once you truly understand how emotions help or hurt you, then you can consciously use the power of emotions to serve you. If you can truly understand the impact of negative emotions, it will be easier for you to make the choice to re-direct these emotions to something positive.

Once I began to recognize the impact of negative emotions on my life, it became easier for me to control these emotions and shift them to my benefit. For instance, I know how jealousy hurts me, and I understand the danger of fear and worry. I saw in my life how negative emotions kept me from exercising my power to achieve what I desired. Therefore, I became committed to transforming these emotions when they showed up because I knew their harm. I am not saying that I got rid of these emotions completely. That is impossible, because as humans we were built to experience both the positive and the negative. Instead, I was able to reduce the duration of negativity and refocus the energy on positive or productive feelings and actions. Sometimes this was easy and sometimes it took a lot more effort. The level of effort I was willing to put in depended on how badly I wanted to move forward versus being stuck where I was. Remember, emotions are energy and negative emotions are negative energy. Negative energy will always create a block to your positive desires.

This chapter focuses specifically on four very powerful emotions – fear, jealousy, love, and gratitude. These emotions either have the power to liberate you or the power to imprison you. The good news is that all emotional energy can be used to your benefit if you are aware of its powers and know how to work with the energy. This chapter will help you understand the creative power of these emotions and how to use them or transform them to always support you. You will find that managing and consciously directing your emotions is a practice and a discipline. The more you make the effort to move your inner energy towards that which makes you feel good and in balance, the more powerful you become.

"I saw that I am stronger than fear."

~**Malala Yousafzai**
(Pakistani activist)

Fear

There is a lot written about the negative effects of fear in creating what you desire. The bottom line is that fear is a paralyzing emotion, keeping you stuck where you are and preventing you from taking any kind of action. Have you ever woken up in the middle of the night from a strange noise and been frozen in fear? If you know the threat is real, you automatically take action to protect yourself. If you don't know the threat is real, you stay paralyzed. Most of the time, the fear we feel is not real or an immediate threat. As a result, this emotion keeps us paralyzed and no real action is taken. You stay where you are and nothing really changes.

I was able to grasp the paralyzing impact of fear and the

benefits of eliminating fear through sport. I am basically a self-taught downhill skier, but I have managed to get pretty good at it through mental and physical practice. I love challenging runs and the feeling of successfully skiing down a very tough trail. I remember times of being at the top of a double black diamond trail looking down and feeling scared. While I wanted to go down the slope successfully, my whole body would be paralyzed in fear. If I tried to ski with any sense of fear, I would fall constantly on the way down. I could never achieve my goal of successfully skiing down the mountain if I was afraid. The moment I eliminated fear and focused on my goal of how I wanted to feel skiing down, I would have the most incredible run. It was like magic. Specifically, I consciously stopped any negative thoughts of future outcomes (the fear of falling or hitting a tree), and I set an intention with a vision of what I wanted to accomplish, and how I wanted to feel (good). On the way down, I only focused on what I was doing in the moment. I knew that the instant I felt fear, I would lose my focus and fall. I know in skiing or in life, fear will either stop me or make me fall or fail unless I move through fear by shifting to a determined focus on what I desire.

If your fear is not an indication of an immediate threat, then your fear is not real. It is a barrier in your mind that you need to break through. It is the gatekeeper to your dreams and desires. Once you recognize your fear, you need to move through it with a feeling of confidence and commitment in order to reach your goals. It will always be your choice as to whether you let fear stop you or not. Your desires need to be stronger than your fears in order for you to move through the gate of fear. If my desire to ski down the double back diamond trail was not stronger than my fear, then I would have turned back and taken an easier run. Your fears will always test the strength of your desires.

Therefore, make your desires stronger than your fears. Your fear is not real, but your heart filled desires are. Focus on what is in your heart.

"The fear habit is very detrimental because you attract the things you fear. If we have any fear we need to get rid of it."
~Peace Pilgrim
(spiritual teacher and activist, 1908-1981)

Another harmful result of fear is that whatever you persistently fear will manifest in your life. I know this is not easy to hear, but it is true. If you fear you will fall down the ski slope, you will. If you fear that you will fail, you will. If you persistently fear you will get sick, you will. If you fear someone will harm you or be hostile towards you, then that will be your experience. Remember, fear is an emotion that is tied to a thought, and thoughts create. Fear is a very powerful negative emotion, and if it persists, it will create what you fear. If you feed your fear with the power of added thoughts and words, you give your fear even more power to create. Therefore, if you want something, then don't fear it. If you don't want something, then don't fear it. If you want a new job, don't fear you won't get one. If you want to be in a relationship, don't fear you won't be in one. If you want to be successful at anything, don't fear you are not good enough. If you want to have a peaceful life, don't fear conflict and chaos. Know that fear creates.

When you feel fear inside of you, understand what you are really fearing. Ask yourself: What am I fearing? Is fear holding me back or hurting me? Do I want to experience what I am fearing? Get to know your fears so you can identify your enemy. Know that feeling fear is a choice. You can decide not to let fear stop you, hurt you, or hold you back. You can do this by consciously moving away from fear and shifting the energy into something productive that is aligned with your goals. For example, when I ski, I move from a fear of falling to a focus on skiing. This can apply to anything you are doing – writing a book, starting a new business, making a big presentation, caring for someone who is sick. When fear creeps in, acknowledge it as an indication that it is time to get seriously focused. Stay focused on your writing, building your business, learning a new skill, gaining new knowledge, or anything that benefits you and keeps you feeling good. Even if it takes more time to shift your emotional energy, by making the effort, you are slowing down the manifestations of your fears. Therefore, do not fear if you are still not completely over your fear! If your intent is to stop your fear, then your intention plus your efforts have already started to help you move towards what you want.

> *"If you want to conquer fear, don't sit home and think about it. Go out and get busy."*
>
> ~**Dale Carnegie**
> **(American writer, 1888-1955)**

Six weeks after I lost my job, I joined my husband on his work trip to Portugal. I had three days by myself to explore the city and enjoy life. On the first night there, I could not sleep. I woke up paralyzed in fear. I felt an incredibly strong fear of not having any income. I had never lost my job before and I was suddenly experiencing a high level of anxiety. Being in a foreign country probably added to my anxiety. I hated how I was feeling. I could barely breathe. I tried meditating, but I couldn't clear my mind. I decided to get out of bed and leave the hotel to distract myself. I spent the day exploring the city, which eased my feelings of fear. I re-read chapters of a self-help book to get myself centered and back in a calmer state of mind. I stayed active the whole trip, so on the last day my fears had subsided. The initial paralyzing feeling of fear on the first day was so strong and debilitating I knew I had to get out of that state immediately. I knew the dangers of unsubstantiated fear and I was committed to never feel that way again. Every time fear crept back in, I consciously stopped it or shifted it to focus and even excitement as quickly as possible. I went out and explored different parts of the city, went on tours, and met some great people. When I shifted fear into something productive, I experienced the joy of living.

Overall, understand that fear has the power to paralyze you and stop you from reaching the dreams that live in your heart. It also has the ability to hurt you and create unwanted experiences. You have the power to decide not to feel prolonged fear. You have the power to consciously pass through your fears by shifting your perspective and your focus. Shifting the energy of fear into something productive that supports your desires is one of the most powerful strategies you can have to create your positive reality. The quicker you can shift out of fear, the quicker and easier (with ease versus with suffering) you will achieve the life or the outcome you desire. Practice moving through your fears and harnessing the energy to push you forward into your positive desires. By doing so you will see how powerful you are.

"Fear is not real. It is a product of thoughts you create. Do not misunderstand me. Danger is very real. But fear is a Choice."

~Will Smith
(Hollywood actor)

There are lesser degrees of fear, which are also harmful. These emotions are anxiety, nervousness, and worry. The base of these emotions is fear. Therefore, the same thing holds true – what you fear will manifest in your life unless you shift these feelings into something that serves you. Anxiety and nervousness are powerful emotions that can completely shift your whole being and behavior. For example, I remember the first time I was asked to speak in front of two hundred people. It was our monthly company meeting and my boss at the time thought it would be a good development opportunity for me to present the business financials to the company in place of him. I was flattered yet terrified. I was so anxious and nervous leading up to the actual presentation. When I started to speak, I could hear my voice shutter and shake. I kept getting more nervous, which made me completely forget what I was supposed to say. I even froze and went silent for a few moments, which felt like an eternity. I finally managed to get myself back together to finish my presentation; however, overall it was a disaster. From that experience, I learned the debilitating nature of being overly nervous and anxious. Since that time, I have had many other opportunities to present to a large number of people. I started to get better at it as soon as I learned to shift my nervousness to focus. I started to actually enjoy it when I shifted my nervousness and anxiety to excitement. I found it is not much of a leap to shift anxiety to excitement. The feelings in the body are similar, and the only difference is your state of mind. The next time you feel anxious, tell yourself you are excited and see what happens.

Worry is an interesting emotion because some believe it is a positive emotion. For example, parents worry about their children because they care about them. However, worry is still a negative emotion and, as such, it still creates a negative vibration that focuses your energy on what you fear may happen. Instead of worry, shift it to belief in what you want. If you are worried you will fail, shift it to a belief that you will succeed. If you are worried you will get sick, then shift the feeling to a belief that you will take care of your health. If someone you love worries for you because they care about you, tell them to believe in you instead. Worry is harmful regardless of whether you think the intent is positive. You need to focus your energy always on what you do want versus what you don't want. Do not worry. Shift worry to belief or faith in something positive.

When you find yourself in states of fear, anxiety or worry, remember you are aligning your creative powers to what you do not want. Think of these feelings as your cosmic warning signal that your inner world is not aligned with your desires and you need to take action to change a thought or belief. If you find yourself stuck in a state of negative emotion, you can also use the power of words to stop this creative process and shift your creative power into what you do want. Tell yourself, "I am not anxious, I am excited!" "I am not worried, I am confident!" "I am not afraid, I am unstoppable!" The more you hear yourself say the words, the easier it will be to shift yourself into a positive creative alignment. When you can respond to this warning signal in a disciplined, positive, and productive way, you start to master the power of your emotions.

"Beware of jealousy for it verily destroys good deeds the way fire destroys wood."
~**Prophet Mohammad, Hadith 4903**

Jealousy

If I could tell you to stop feeling one emotion

immediately, this would be it. The sole purpose of this emotion is to keep you in suffering and prevent your desire from coming to you. The moment you feel jealousy, you are putting yourself in a vibration that is not aligned with your desires. In other words, you are telling the Universe you do not want what the other person has. In fact, the more you feel jealous, anything you truly desire will be given to others. You will continue to create your desires, but for someone else. This is how this energy works. It's that simple.

If you dissect the emotion of jealousy you will notice that it reflects negative thoughts about oneself and negative thoughts about someone else. For example, if your friend tells you they just got a big promotion, the feelings of jealousy could evoke the thoughts of, "Why didn't that happen to me?" "I am not satisfied where I am today." "He does not deserve it as much as I do." The double negative nature of this emotion creates a much more powerful form of negative energy directed towards oneself. This is why this emotion feels so strong and so bad. None of these negative thoughts serve you, and in fact, they only prevent you from achieving what you desire. The more you feel jealous towards someone, the more of what you desire will be held from you and directed towards that very person you have the jealous feelings towards. Your friend's life will seem to be getting better and better while your life will seem to stay the same.

The key is to recognize your feelings as jealousy as soon as possible and transform that energy into something that accelerates the creation of your personal desires, versus hindering it. To do this you must replace jealousy with a positive supportive emotion, like happiness, immediately. Be happy for that person. If you see something you want that someone else has, then the only way to receive what they have is to put yourself in a positive emotion and vibration. If you want a promotion and your colleague gets one, do not feel jealous of them. If you do, you will block a promotion from coming to you. Instead, be happy for that person. Keep yourself in a positive emotional state or vibration, and at the same time feel positively towards the other person. Even if you don't feel happy, force yourself to say you are happy. Find something good to say. Use the power of your words to create the belief. The more happiness, love or joy you can feel towards something you want that someone else has, the more positive energy you give towards creating what you desire.

If you see someone you know receiving something you desire, look at it as a sign that what you desire is coming to you. It is within your reach. All you need to do in that moment is feel grateful for that sign, for yourself and for the other person. If you desire to be in a relationship and your best friend tells you they have a new boyfriend or girlfriend, use this as an opportunity to accelerate your own desire. Feel happy for your friend within yourself. Feel this way for every person who tells you they just met "the one." Be patient and persistent, and believe the perfect relationship is coming to you.

I learned the negative aspects of jealousy when I was in high school. Growing up, I was jealous of a girl on my street. While I wanted to be her friend, I knew she did not want to be mine. As a result, if anything good happened to her, I felt jealous. I thought she did not deserve the good things and I did. These feelings continued for years. The more I felt jealous, the more my dreams and desires were given to her – from boyfriends to friends and all the other things one cares about in high school. By my senior year, I finally realized what was going on. Even things I imagined in my own head would happen to her exactly how I had imagined them for myself! It was too strange to ignore it as a coincidence. Jealousy was preventing me from manifesting my desires. As a result, I learned about the importance of being happy for others when they received the things I desired. The more I practiced feeling happy for others, the easier it became to feel truly happy instead of jealous. By being happy for others, I opened the energetic gateway to bring my desires into my own life.

Remember, negative emotions do much more damage to you and your experiences than you think. Your emotions are your energetic vibrational state of being and play a significant part in your conscious power to create your reality in a way you desire. Take control of these emotions and direct the energy from the negative vibration to a positive vibration. The higher your emotional vibration, the greater your power to consciously create.

> *"The feeling of love is the highest frequency you can emit. The greater the love you feel and emit, the greater the power you are harnessing."*
>
> ~**Rhonda Byrne**
> (**New Thought author**)

Love

Love is on the highest spectrum of energetic vibration. Love is the greatest force there is, and far greater than the emotions we typically associate with love, such as romantic love, family love, and friendship love. Some say that love is not an emotion at all, but a frequency – the frequency of the Universe or the frequency of Cosmic Consciousness.

Love is how the Universe works – it is unconditional and gives you whatever is a match to what you are thinking and feeling inside. This is why many people say "love is all there is." Being in the frequency of love is being one with your Divine nature. When you tune into the high frequency of love, barriers are broken down, and the path clears its way for you and your true desires to manifest. The love vibration ignites your Divine self and connects you to your highest creative powers. Spiritually, love elevates you to a higher level of consciousness that sits above the negative vibrations. When you are in the vibration of love, you are at your most powerful state of being.

When you are vibrating at the frequency of love, you feel compassionate, tolerant, generous, joyful, and peaceful. Things don't bother you as much and life seems to go easier. You become in the flow of the Universe. This feeling of love is not the kind that is overwhelming or overpowering, in which you feel like you can't think clearly. The frequency of Universal love is balanced, accepting, unconditional, and empowering. It is the emotion and vibration that trumps everything. When you are in the love vibration there is no fear or negative emotions, and there are no barriers in your way. If you truly desire something you will feel the love for it in your heart. The purer the love, the stronger the power to create. By staying in this frequency, you will greatly change your world for the better and you will also change the world for the greater good.

"In the universal sense, love is the divine power of attraction in creation that harmonizes, unites, binds together."
~**Paramahansa Yogananda**
(Indian Yogi/Guru, 1893-1952)

Your greatest power (love) comes from your heart and your soul. It transcends your ego-self. In fact, your ego-self must move out the way and let your soul-self take the lead for you to be your most powerful self. When you create a thought that is tied with the feeling of love, and a belief that it is possible, it will be created in your life. If you follow your deepest desires that live in your heart, you will not fail. What is deep in your heart is who you really are. Many people close their hearts or get distracted by day-to-day routines, never discovering who they really are. Discover what is in your heart and let the power of love pull you towards that reality.

As mentioned earlier, when you stay in the feeling of negative emotions, such as fear or jealousy, you block your desires from being created. You block the vibrations that connect you to your Divine creative powers. If you replace jealous thoughts with loving thoughts, you will automatically shift into your Divine powers. The key is to give love to what you desire, and love the process by which it is manifested. Giving love is being love and being in the high vibration of the Ultimate Creative power. Remember, you are a Divine creator. Your thoughts create. To consciously create your life, your thoughts need to be aligned with your emotions and a true knowing and trust in your ability to create. Your Divine powers come from your spiritual soul-self, which is part of Cosmic Consciousness itself. The more you feel love, the more power you create towards your conscious desire. Being in the love vibration shifts you from being the reactor to your life to the creator you are meant to be.

"Love what you do: Do what you love."
~**Wayne Dyer**
(American philosopher and self-help author)

One of my desires has been to love what I do every day. This desire came about when I started to realize I always looked forward to the weekend and I dreaded Mondays. It seemed insane to me to go through life only living for the weekends. Why couldn't I look forward to every single day? The fact is, I could. Once I decided this was possible and internally shifted my perspective, feeling, and belief, my world molded to my desire. I began loving Mondays as much as Fridays, and my life became far more enjoyable. My work life experiences became less stressful and more fun. You can decide what to love. When you feel love, and give love in your thoughts, words, and actions, you create more love for yourself and others. Your world changes around you.

Staying in the love frequency is not always easy, but it is always a choice. It is a choice to feel positive and to trust in who you are and what is in your heart. Sometimes it is a struggle and an effort to move into the vibration of love. This is when it has to become a practice. You need to become familiar with the feeling of this frequency, so you can identify it when you are tuned in. One way to get yourself in this frequency is to practice noticing what you love every day. I recommend starting with what you love about yourself first, and then move on to other people, places, or things that you love. Ask yourself: "What do I love about myself?" Then ask yourself: "What else do I love?" I made this into a game that I frequently play with my children. Each of us states one thing we love about ourselves for three rounds, then one thing in general that we love – like our dog or vacations in Hawaii – for three rounds. While my daughter finds it easy to say things she loves about herself, my son does not. It is uncomfortable for him. It is easier for him to say what he loves about others or what he loves to do versus what he loves about himself. When my husband plays with us, he struggles in the same way. Many people are like my husband and son in that there is an underlying belief that we should always be looking externally for love, but the truth is, everything starts internally first. Practice loving yourself first even if it feels uncomfortable. Feel what that feels like. Then practice saying what you love in general. Feel what that feels like. Keep doing this until you feel the feeling and power of love within you. You will know the feeling because it will come from your heart.

"When love and spirit are brought together, their power can accomplish anything. Then love, power, and spirit are one."
~**Deepak Chopra (New Thought author)**

Remember you are Divine and you are part of Cosmic Consciousness, the frequency of love. When you are truly tuned in and one with this great power you will feel love towards everyone. You will love all without judgment and you will give love without expecting to receive any back. This is our true spiritual nature. It is the part of ourselves that recognizes and knows that we are all connected. However, most of us are not enlightened and only just beginning to discover this part of ourselves. Therefore, the goal is to keep moving in the direction of the ultimate love vibration. Consciously tune into the feeling of love as often as you can. Open up your heart and see what is inside of you.

"What are you grateful for now? Gratitude can shift your energy, raise your vibration, and make all your next moments even better."

~Joe Vitale
(American author)

Gratitude

The feeling of gratitude is one of the most powerful and positive energetic forces in the creation process. It has the ability to create your desires if it is used consciously and correctly. It is the gateway to the ultimate love vibration. When you are feeling grateful for someone or something you feel a deep sense of joy, happiness, and humility. You feel a love and appreciation for what you have and for the source of what you have. There is a dual positive nature to gratitude. When someone gives you a gift, you feel happy for the gift you received and you feel happiness towards the person who gave you the gift. Similarly, when it comes to people, things, or circumstances in your life that you are grateful for, you first feel an inner sense of happiness and positivity for what you have, and then you give this energy to something greater, in deep appreciation. There is first an inward vibration of positive energy, and then an external giving of positive energy. This exchange of positive energy is a language in the Universe. The positive vibration of gratitude attracts and creates more of what you are grateful for. With the emotion and vibration of gratitude, two positives create magic.

"A grateful mind is a great mind which eventually attracts to itself great things."

~Plato
(Greek philosopher, 428-348 BC)

Magic is the ability to influence the course of events by harnessing spiritual forces. Gratitude is the key to creating magic in your life because it aligns you towards the power of love. Gratitude puts you in a vibration that aligns you with the universal forces that support what you are grateful for. The good news is, it is easy to feel gratitude. There is always something to be grateful for, whether it is your health, your family, your friends, clean air, or freedom. However, in our busy lives, it is easy to take things for granted. We are so busy that we don't stop to think about what we are grateful for. We are constantly striving to get by or get ahead, providing for ourselves and our families. By focusing only on what we want versus what we already have, we put ourselves out of energetic balance and unconsciously misuse our energetic powers. Our energy then gets directed more towards what we don't have versus towards what we do have.

You can think of gratitude as an energetic practice and discipline. By practicing gratitude, you condition your body to be in a state of higher vibration. You feel good more often. You start to harness the power of love, because much of what you are grateful for are the things you love. When you are in a state of gratitude for what you have, you are happy in that moment for something the way it is right now. You shift your energy into a positive vibration and a higher frequency. Gratitude is the quickest way to help you reach a positive vibration because it immediately makes you feel good. When you first start to consciously practice being grateful for what you have, it may feel unnatural to you or hard because it is not something you consciously think about. Start small and be grateful for the little things in your life, then let your mind continue to find more big and small things that you are grateful for. The goal is to raise your creative vibration and align your inner being to the positive parts of your life. Take the time to stop, refocus, and rebalance your inner being in order to be in your most powerful state. Find a time of day that works best for you and write down everything you are grateful for. Practice writing down or saying out loud what you are grateful for every day. Keep doing this until your mind is automatically grateful. There are many useful techniques in practicing gratitude, including keeping a gratitude journal or doing a thirty-day gratitude challenge. Find the strategy that works best for you, which keeps you in a disciplined practice. You will find that you become happier and you start to attract more positive things into your life.

"What you focus on expands, and when you focus on the goodness in your life, you create more of it."
~Oprah Winfrey (Media proprietor)

When you get in a feeling of appreciation or love for what is, you detach from the feeling of striving for what is not yet. This is an incredibly important aspect of this emotion. With the feeling of gratitude, you release any feeling of unease in your body, and you align yourself with a feeling of grateful acceptance, which opens you up energetically to receive more. Gratitude removes energy barriers that block, slow down, or stop the positive creation process. Therefore, the magic of gratitude not only directs positive energy towards what you are grateful for, but it also removes energetic barriers, preventing you from creating and receiving what you do not yet have. I will explain more about the importance of detaching from the feeling of striving when consciously creating your reality in the next chapter.

Being grateful for what is does not mean you will stop creating more. Don't be afraid of being grateful for what is and feel like you are telling the Universe you are satisfied with everything in your life and you do not want any more. Your Divine nature is that of a creator. You are here to experience who you are. The world around you is constantly changing and creating new things. It is your nature to constantly create new experiences. Gratitude grounds your energy and redirects it into the vibration of positive creation. Like any good magician, it takes practice to learn how to harness and direct energy to influence an outcome. Therefore, practice gratitude as often as you can. Feel the difference in your body between when you feel grateful for what is and when you strive for what you don't have yet. Get to know the difference in feeling. See what happens when you are in the state of gratitude. Begin to notice how your emotional powers feel and how they influence your life.

The hidden secret of gratitude is that its power can be applied to what you desire even if you do not yet have it. The key is to feel grateful for what you desire before you even receive it. The feeling of gratitude creates an internal vibrational alignment with the Universe. You communicate through this energetic field that you are in alignment with what you want. Gratitude is the magic ingredient when you consciously create your reality. Gratitude is the feeling that includes the underlying knowing that there are spiritual forces working on your behalf for the achievement of your desires. Therefore, be grateful for all that you have and all that you desire. Feel like you have already received what you desire and express your appreciation accordingly. Express gratitude with the same feeling you feel when you feel grateful for something you already have. Feel it authentically. Gratitude must come from the heart in order for it to be true. Therefore, to be truly grateful for what you don't have yet you must have a deep sense of faith, trust, and belief in the spiritual forces that work on your behalf. You feel grateful for what you don't have yet because you have an inner knowing that it must come to you. When you feel from this place then you have unlocked the secret to gratitude.

******

All emotions are energy and have power. You can either be controlled by your emotions or you can control your emotions and use their power to support you. It can be easy for our emotions to control us, especially when we feel strong negative emotions. The energy in negative emotions propels us to react and feed the negative energy, and it holds us back from being our powerful selves. You must become more aware of your emotions and how they make you feel, so you can become the master of your emotional energy. Feel your emotions, but do not immediately react to them. Understand what your emotions are telling you, and then consciously move the energy from feeling negative into something that supports you – for example, a positive feeling, a positive action, or positive words. Understand the spiritual and creative impact emotions play in your life. Channel negative energy into positive energy that is directed to what you want to create in your life. Consciously practice creating positive emotional states through gratitude and love, so you can raise your vibration and become a more powerful creator of your life and your world. Let your emotions become your guide to creating a positive vibratory state of your inner world, so you can experience a positive life in your outer world.

The Power of Feelings

1. Emotions are life energy inside of you. Emotional energy is an extension of your thought energy. It is your body's response to a thought that you physically feel.

2. Energetically, not all emotions are created equal. Negative emotions are low vibrating negative energy, whereas positive emotions are high vibrating positive energy. The higher the energetic vibration, the stronger your positive creative powers will be; therefore, keep your emotions positive.

3. Fear has the power to paralyze you and stop you from fulfilling the dreams that live in your heart. It also has the ability to hurt you and create unwanted or feared experiences. What you persistently fear will manifest.

4. Anxiety, nervousness, and worry are lesser degrees of fear. Therefore, the same thing holds true – what you fear will manifest in your life unless you shift your energy towards something positive.

5. When you feel negative emotions in your body, consciously shift your energy into something productive or positive. Do not let the emotion persist. Shift fear to focus, anxiety to excitement, and worry to belief.

6. Jealousy is a destructive emotion. Do not feel it. Energetically, jealousy will keep your desires away from you, and will continue to give to others the very things you desire.

7. Love in the purest form is the vibration and frequency of Cosmic Consciousness. Love is

unconditional, giving, balanced, peaceful, and accepting. The closer you get to the vibration of love, the more powerful of a creator you will become.

8. Gratitude is the gateway to the ultimate vibration of love. The feeling of gratitude attracts into your life more of what you are grateful for.

9. The hidden secret of gratitude is that its power can be applied to what you have and to what you desire even if you do not yet have it. The key is to feel grateful for what you desire before you receive it.

10. By consistently practicing the feelings of gratitude and love, you condition your body to be in a state of high vibration. You feel good and your world changes for the better.

Chapter Six

How to Create

"What the mind of man can conceive and believe, it can achieve."

~Napoleon Hill
(American author, 1883-1970)

It is your birthright to be a conscious creator, because it is who you are and why you are here. Believe it or not, you have the same creative power and abilities as anyone on this planet, including the most powerful world leader, the most successful businessman, artist, or scientist. This chapter will explain to you how to consciously create your desires, so you can discover for yourself how powerful you truly are. In order to consciously create anything that you desire, the process is always the same. The only difference is the length of time it may take to manifest what you desire. It is important to understand that conscious creation is a process and there are specific steps needed in order to create most efficiently.

The Creation Process:

1. Create a clear conscious thought, desire, or intention

2. Express gratitude as if you have received it

3. Detach from your desire

4. Align your actions with your desire

The key to being able to successfully move through

each step is your ability to believe and trust in the spiritual forces that support you. In other words, you need to align your inner energy to a vibration that attracts what you desire. Notice that steps one through three are internal requirements, and step four is external. This means that before you take action, you must first see it in your mind, feel it, believe it, and trust that it already is. The truth is, often this is easier said than done due to our conditioned tendencies, fears, or doubts. This is why it is important for you to clearly understand the requirements of each step in the process, and train yourself through discipline and practice. The more you understand and practice, the better you will get at consciously creating your life. This chapter will elaborate more on the creation process by providing additional tools, strategies, and examples to help you in your process.

"Once you make a decision the universe conspires to make it happen."

-Ralph Waldo Emerson
(American essayist, 1803-1882)

Step 1: Create a Clear Conscious Thought, Desire, or Intention

As I mentioned earlier in the book, a conscious thought is a thought that is aligned with your positive desire with the added power of feeling and belief. Creating a conscious thought is easy when your desire is already clear in your mind, and is backed by an inner belief that it is possible. Typically, your belief is already established because it is based on your prior experiences or established evidence. Creating a conscious thought takes more time and effort when you want to create something you have not experienced before or something different than what your external reality is currently showing you. You cannot move beyond step one until you can see, feel, and believe your desire.

Your first step in the creation process is for you to see and feel the end goal in your mind, which means you need to establish a vision. In creating a vision, it is important to get as clear as possible on the outcome. This does not mean you need all the details worked out. Actually, you should not be focusing on all the details. You need to get as clear as possible on the end goal and know exactly what you want to achieve. Be able to articulate for yourself what you want or where you are going. Without a vision, there is no destination. For example, if you put nothing into a navigation system, then you don't get a route to follow because the navigation system does not know where you are going. Your vision is your destination. It is your job to state the destination and then take the route that is presented to you. In other words, at the start of the creation process know WHAT you want, but don't get hung up on the HOW. Your first step is only on knowing the WHAT.

"Create a vision of who you want to be, and then live into it as if it were already true."

~Arnold Schwarzenegger
(former Governor of California)

When I wanted to improve my skiing, I would observe skiers who were better than me and visualize in my head what it would feel like to ski that way. I would see it in my mind and feel it in my body. This was how I significantly improved my skiing abilities. It always began with a vision of what I wanted to achieve. Similarly, when I was hired to build a finance team I knew I needed a vision of what success would look and feel like when I had accomplished what I was hired to do. I created a vision in my mind of a team of people who were trusted partners, advisors, and drivers of the business. I knew what my destination looked like and felt like, and I was confident I could achieve my goal. Within two years, I achieved more than I originally envisioned. Step one is always to see it, feel it, and believe it.

If the vision is not clear and there is no positive emotional connection to it, then it will not manifest. I have seen this in the corporate world when leaders fail to achieve their goals because their vision is unclear, hollow, or uninspired. When this happens, the leader fails to build belief in the people who are hired to help achieve the goal. More specifically, when there is confusion about the vision in the workplace, then conflict arises, tensions build, work becomes difficult, and things do not move forward. There is a lot of energy spent, but it is mostly wasted. I have seen organizations break apart because there was no aligned clear vision of the destination. This holds true in all aspects of your life. If you don't take the time to create a clear vision for where you are going and a belief you can get there, then you will not get there.

"Reality leaves a lot to the imagination."
~John Lennon
(singer-songwriter)

It may take time to formulate your vision and that is okay. The bigger the change in your life the longer it may take to formulate your vision. However, if you strongly desire a change then you need to spend the time and effort on creating your vision, and understanding what you truly desire in your heart. Fortunately, you have tools and access to spiritual resources that can help you to create a clear vision. Remember, you are a spiritual being connected to the source of everything. One of your spiritual and creative tools is your imagination. Use your imagination to create an image in your mind of what you would like to create. If you want to create prosperity, what does that look like to you? What does it feel like? If you want to create peace, a loving relationship, a successful business – what does that look and feel like? Use your imagination in the way it is meant to be used, which is to create. Everything ever created came from someone's imagination. Therefore, practice using it. Unfortunately, many of us have been conditioned out of using our imagination unless you have made a career as an artist, writer, musician, or inventor. When I grew up I was never told about the importance or power of the imagination. I thought imagination was just fantasy in my head or something I used when I would play. The truth is, your imagination is your ability to create new ideas, images, or concepts in your mind that are outside of what has already been created. Once you hold the image in your mind with feeling and belief, you start the process of creation. Ask yourself: "When was the last time I really used my imagination?"

"Your imagination is your preview of life's coming attractions."

~**Albert Einstein**
(theoretical physicist, 1879-1955)

Oftentimes, in order to imagine the possibilities, you need to receive some form of inspiration. Inspiration is the process by which you stimulate your mind to consciously connect with information and ideas outside of your limited ego-mind. Inspiration is the process of consciously connecting to Cosmic Consciousness. All artists need some form of inspiration in order to create. Inspiration can come from anywhere. You are the best person to determine what form of inspiration you need. For big life changes, some people go to personal development conferences or workshops, travel, spend time in nature, look at art, tour beautiful places, meet new people, read books or magazines, meditate, and so on. When you are creating your life, inspiration is part of the creative process. Inspiration opens your mind up to new things and new ideas which help to formulate your vision of what you want. One common practice to help create a vision and hold it in your mind is to create a vision board. By pulling together pictures from magazines or the internet that inspire you and reflect your true desires, you begin to formulate and cement your vision in your mind.

"Create the highest grandest vision possible for your life, because you become what you believe."

~Oprah Winfrey
(media proprietor)

Once you have your vision in place, and you know where you want to go, you need to believe you can get there. Belief is the foundation of all conscious creation. You might create a beautiful vision in your mind, but without the belief that it is possible, it is just a daydream. You need to believe in your vision, otherwise it has no creative power. If your vision has conviction, then your vision must manifest. The quickest way to determine if you believe in your vision is to feel if you have any doubt. If doubt is present then you do not have a strong belief. As mentioned earlier in this book, all beliefs can be changed because beliefs are perspectives and not truths.

When you are looking to make changes in your life that are different than your experiences, then belief becomes the biggest hurdle to overcome. If you want something different for yourself, you need to create the belief that it is possible, despite all past conditioning. If you don't yet believe in your vision, analyze why you don't believe. If you want something to change badly enough then put all your effort into changing your belief. Any belief can be changed and any new belief can be created. Some changes happen quickly and other changes take longer because you are having to address a deeper or core belief about yourself. There are many resources available to help you identify and change your limiting core beliefs. When I wanted to make a career change, I knew the one thing I needed was the belief I could actually do it. I did whatever it took to build a new positive belief in myself. I read multiple books, went on retreats, and turned to others who served as mentors or coaches. I was committed to building the belief in myself because I knew without belief nothing was going to change. Building a new belief about yourself, like learning anything new, takes time and commitment. In other words, it takes practice, focus, and discipline to change your internal makeup.

"By believing passionately in something that still does not exist, we create it. The nonexistent is whatever we have not sufficiently desired."

~Franz Kafka
(novelist, 1883-1924)

Often, we limit ourselves with what we see and know, which is currently in our lives. We think we only live in a physical world and we forget we live in a spiritual world too. As mentioned earlier, the spiritual world creates the physical world. Therefore, you need to work with the unseen before it becomes seen. In other words, you need to believe it before you see it. Unfortunately, most of us were taught the opposite, that seeing is believing. You must understand that everything you experience starts with what is inside of you. Create a new world by first creating it within yourself. Create the vision, feel the vision, and believe it is possible. The thought, feeling, and belief all have to be aligned. This is what starts the creative process, and what commands the universal forces to work on your behalf.

Step 2: Express Gratitude as if You Have Already Received It

In chapter five, I discussed that gratitude is the magic ingredient when you consciously create your reality. The key is to feel grateful for what you desire before you receive it. The feeling of gratitude is powerful because it creates an internal vibrational alignment in the Universe with that which you are grateful for. When you feel gratitude for something before you receive it, you have faith that you already have it in the unseen and that it will soon manifest in the seen. You trust that there are spiritual and energetic forces working on your behalf. Feeling and expressing gratitude is the easiest way to align your inner world at the energetic and vibrational level with your desires. Therefore, in the creation process, once you have created your conscious desire, feel like you already have what you desire and be grateful for it. Say "thank you" for your desire regularly.

"See the things you want as already yours."
~**Rhonda Byrne**
(New Thought author)

Sometimes it may be hard to embody the feeling of already having something, especially if you are desiring something very different from what you are currently experiencing. This is when you need to use your imagination to really feel it, and then be grateful for it.

Step 3: Detach from Your Desire

Once you have established your conscious thought or vision with belief and gratitude, it is time to get out of the way and let the universal forces guide and support you. You need to give the universal creative energies time to bring your vision into your reality. The time your desire will take to manifest will depend on what is being created, because everything has its own time. Some things take as little as one hour or one day to manifest, while others can take months or years. I cannot tell you how long it will take, but I can tell you how not to slow the process down so that it keeps operating in the most efficient manner. Eventually, you will be able to sense for yourself how much time it will take. More times than not, you will experience that the universal forces of Cosmic Consciousness exceed your expectations and things happen faster than you imagined.

"Relinquish your attachment to the known, step into the unknown, and you will step into the field of all possibilities."

~**Deepak Chopra**
(New Thought author)

To create with ease and efficiency, you must detach from your vision. This means you must not constantly strive for it or want it. You must not hold onto your vision in desperation, with fear of letting it go. You *need* to let it go. This is a very important concept to understand and it is a critical step to creating with ease. Detaching can be very hard to do, especially if you believe that if you let go of thinking into your desires then they will not manifest. Many people believe that by constantly hoping and wishing for something, they can bring it to life. This is absolutely not true. You cannot mentally force something to happen. When you strive internally, your body and feelings are in a state of unease. When you are in unease, you are only creating more unease in your reality. The more unease you feel, the longer and more difficult the manifestation process is, because you are not vibrationally aligned with your positive desires. Remember that feeling any strain or stress is a negative emotion and a low vibration. When you feel unease then you are no longer tuned into the positive creative energy of your desires. Therefore, you need to tune back into the right frequency by moving out of the negative emotion. In order to create easily, your body needs to feel a sense of gratitude, peace, confidence, calm, and faith that whatever the outcome, it will be the best one possible. When you are detached, you are no longer putting any mental strain against your desire. You have trust in the process and take action based on where your instincts guide you.

Your inner feelings will always be your guide in letting you know if you have successfully detached or not, because attachment is a feeling. The root emotion of attachment is fear. When you stay emotionally and energetically attached to something, you do so because you are afraid of losing something. Remember that fear is paralyzing and it blocks you from achieving your desires. Attachment keeps you in the low vibration of fear. When you detach, you release any negative emotions within you, and you allow for the creative process to happen. Another emotional indicator of attachment is the feeling of disappointment. Feeling disappointment stops the creative process immediately. Disappointment is a feeling you have when you do not get what you desire in the way you may have wanted it. Understand there are unlimited ways of achieving your desire. There is always another way, so there is never a reason to feel disappointment. Instead, accept any unwanted situation without any negative feelings and trust in your creative process. Try transforming the emotion of disappointment into focus and see what happens. You will likely rediscover your own power to create.

"Nonresistance is the key to the greatest power in the universe."

~Eckhart Tolle
(spiritual author)

There is a difference between wanting something and having an intention. The biggest difference is in the feeling associated with want, compared to the feeling of actually having. When the feeling of want persists, you are in a state of attachment. The feeling of want is usually a feeling that you are grasping for something and trying to control an outcome. It is an uneasy feeling, because it is a constant striving for something you are lacking. With the feeling of want there is doubt and no trust that there is a larger cosmic energy working for you and through you. Your energy is constantly being directed to the thought of lack. If you keep putting energy and thought into "wanting" something, you will continue to experience "wanting" something. Therefore, KNOW what you desire and stop wanting it. In the spiritual realm, when you set an intention, you are giving the universal energy an order that it will begin to execute. The forces start to organize and bring what you intend into form. When you feel want, the universal forces stop organizing. The feeling counteracts the intention. You will never get what you want until you release the feeling of "wanting." Instead, trust you will receive in Divine and perfect timing.

> "Everything you want is coming. Relax and let the universe pick the timing and the way. You just need to trust that what you want is coming, and watch how fast it comes."
>
> ~**Abraham Hicks**
> **(New Thought author and speaker)**

When you shift from the feeling of want to trust, you automatically let go. If you have done it before, you know how it feels. You are able to easily move on to other things, you know when and what actions to take, and there is never a moment when you feel fear or doubt. You operate from a place of calm, focus, and knowing. If you find yourself struggling to trust and detach, there are a few different strategies that can help you.

- Have the perspective that it will happen in the exact way it is meant to happen. From this perspective, you will no longer worry about the outcome. This puts you in the feeling of trust.

- Fake it before you make it. You have probably heard this saying before. In truth, there is a lot of wisdom to it. By faking that you already have your desire, you start to build a feeling that you already have something. Over time, the feeling of having is truly established and you detach from a feeling of wanting something. You need to use your imagination to picture in your mind and feel in your body that you already have what you desire. Similarly, begin to "act as if" you already have what you desire. Adjust your attitudes and actions to be aligned as much as is reasonable with your desires.

- Embrace the unknown and develop a positive feeling to uncertainty. In the space of uncertainty is all possibility. Learn to love the feeling of not knowing what is next. Let it excite you and make you feel like anything is possible.

- When fear or doubt creeps in, remember to shift these emotions into something productive. Focus on something that serves you and moves you in the direction of your desire or goal. Make sure what you are focused on is making you feel good.

Step 4: Align Your Actions with Your Desire

When you detach, you allow the spiritual forces to work on your behalf and bring into physical form what you desire. Depending on what you desire, it may manifest quickly or you may need to take action as part of the creation process. By the time you have reached step four, you have already aligned yourself internally towards your desire with faith that it will be created. At this stage, the hard work is already done. Any action that follows needs to be aligned with your desire. You and only you will know what, if anything, you need to do next. The actions you are guided to take will feel right to you. It is only when you have not completed the first three steps that action feels hard, you waste time and energy, and you do not feel like you are getting anywhere. In this part of the process you need to trust yourself and the spiritual forces that support you. The following represent different forms of action taken in the final step.

- No action: Sometimes you will find that no action is required. You have already taken the action to align yourself internally with your desire and you have successfully attracted into your reality what you desired.

- Follow your instincts: This is when you need to let your heart be your guide. Your instincts will tell you what you need to do next to create your desires. You will experience the universal forces bringing things to you, people to you, and opportunities to you for further action. Follow the flow of where you are being led.

- Be persistent: You need to keep moving forward, taking the necessary actions with commitment and a strong belief that you will achieve what you desire. The longer it takes, the more you are being challenged to grow and learn in the process. Therefore, when you finally achieve your goals, you have achieved so much more. Do not give up.

- Be the change: All your words and actions need to be aligned with your desire. Your words and actions are a reflection of what is inside of you. Be conscious of what you say and do and make sure your words and actions are aligned with who you want to be or what you want to see in the world.

Creation in Action

Remember, you are creating all the time. You are an incredible human being with a multitude of thoughts, feeling, and beliefs housed in your being. Your reality is always reflecting what is inside of you. You create the future with what is inside you today. In every moment, you have the opportunity to create what you desire. So, pick your big moments and pick your small moments, and practice shifting how you view and interact in this world. The more you experience how this process works for yourself, the more powerful you will become as a creator of your reality.

One of my big moments of conscious creation was when I decided I wanted to move across the country and reach the level of chief financial officer. I had a vision, I felt it, and believed in it, and I detached from the outcome. When the desire was strongly planted in my mind with conviction, the Universe started to support me. I was guided to take unusual steps in my career and I faced challenging circumstances, but I knew it was all happening for my benefit. It took two years to achieve my goal, but that was two years sooner than I thought. Once you believe in yourself, trust you will get there no matter what. Do not be attached to the outcome and do not doubt that your desire will manifest. Your path for bigger life changes will always have both positive and negative turns, but use both forms of energy to your benefit. Be grateful for the positive circumstances and see the negative situations as a benefit or opportunity. The perceived negative circumstances will always be the ones that accelerate your journey towards your desire or goal.

One of my smaller but highly powerful moments of creation was a family ski trip to Park City, Utah. My intention and desire was for this trip to be an amazing family vacation where everyone had a great time skiing and experiencing all the aspects of everything I love about Park City (restaurants, my favorite after ski spot, ice skating, and so on). For several years, we would plan ski trips out West, which were less than ideal as the mountains would be pretty dry with not much snow. In fact, two years prior, we planned a trip to Whistler, BC, and there was barely any snow. We could only ski the top half of the mountain because there was literally only mud and rock on the bottom half. After that trip, we took a year off from skiing feeling it was not worth risking our time and money if we were going to experience another dry season. Despite our prior experiences, I was determined to head back out West and get the kids on skis again. While my husband was nervous about the trip and the predicted unfavorable weather conditions, I held to my vision and belief of a great vacation. I truly detached from the outcome of the trip and went into the trip without "wanting" anything. When we landed in Salt Lake City, it was raining and sixty degrees (not the best temperature for good ski conditions) yet I was not disappointed. I pictured again in my head what I desired – great skiing – and I felt it, and detached. When we woke up the next morning at the ski resort, the rain storm had turned into a snow storm overnight. While the weather forecast predicted four inches of new snow, we got eighteen inches of new snow. The ski conditions were the best I had experienced in at least ten years. The snow fall was predicted to continue for the remainder of the week. After the second day of skiing, even though we were enjoying the snow fall, I wanted to experience a sunny day before we went home. In reality, there was nothing to make me believe this was possible. However, I decided to do the same manifestation process – think and feel it in a vision, believe it, and detach (this literally took me 20 seconds). Well, the next day at around 1 p.m., the skies cleared and the sun came out. The weather app on my iPhone still said it was cloudy. So yes, you can control the weather. This is the power you have at your disposal! This might sound unbelievable to you, but your energy impacts everything outside of you. I shared this example to exemplify how you can unlock your own power in your everyday life.

"The world can only change from within."

~**Eckhart Tolle**
(spiritual author)

The Power of Non-Resistance in the Creation Process

There is an underlying vibration you must maintain in order to successfully create your positive desires. You are at your most powerful when you are in a constant state of non-resistance. When you resist, you create energetic friction and you put up barriers to achieving and manifesting your life desires. Resistance holds a negative vibration and weakens your creative powers. Resistance is a feeling within you. Even if you think you are resisting something unrelated to your desire, the feeling of resistance within you impacts everything. The reason this is so, is because everything inside of you – your thoughts, feelings, and beliefs, create your external reality. For example, if you are irritated about something and it persists, you will find more things start to show up that irritate you and fuel that feeling. This is the same with the feeling of resistance. When you resist one thing and that feeling persists, you block the positive creative energy flow and other parts of your life are impacted in a negative way.

Do not resist what is, even if you are not happy with what is. In the process of manifestation, you will always experience things that can either be perceived as negative or positive. Accept what you perceive as negative and do not resist it. Accept it and know you have the power to change it. On my ski trip to Park City, I did not feel resistance in the form of disappointment when my weather app told me it was going to rain or stay cloudy. Instead, I decided to create the reality I desired. I went inside myself, created a vision of what I desired, and detached from it with gratitude.

Releasing resistance is powerful in all situations. Sometimes, you may not know you are holding resistance in your body. For three years, I resisted letting people know I wore a wig due to an immune disorder called alopecia. I thought people would see me as less than, so I did everything I could to make my hair look natural, so no one would know. When I finally told my work colleagues my secret, I felt exposed and vulnerable. I wondered if it really mattered that they knew. But as time passed, I realized I experienced a sense of internal ease by telling my colleagues the truth, which allowed for greater confidence, new experiences, and new relationships that were greater than I had ever experienced before.

Resistance is an internal fighting against what is. For some reason, we believe we are protecting ourselves by internally pushing against what we do not like. This is similar to the feeling of wanting when we are internally grasping for something we don't have. With resistance, we are afraid to surrender to what is because we are afraid we will continue to receive what it is we do not like. The shortest way to change what you don't like is to first accept it. You need to get out of the feeling of resisting what is.

It is the feeling or energetic vibration that is holding you back. Acceptance releases the vibration of resistance. From that place of acceptance, you then have the power to create something new. Once you release resistance, you open the gateway for the powerful spiritual forces of Cosmic Consciousness to more consistently support the creation of your desires in the physical world.

Oftentimes, you build up the vibration of resistance if you are hiding something about yourself, have strong negative feelings towards someone, or blame someone for something in your life. Holding resentment is holding resistance. If you want to clear your energetic path way to maximize your creative powers and your spiritual abilities, you should identify any area of resistance (or negative emotion) in your life and work on releasing it. By clearing even one path, you will open yourself up to greater creative energy. You will know when you have successfully released resistance because you will feel lighter.

Ways to release resistance:

- Accept what is

- Release resentment

- Forgive someone for what they have done

- Admit your secret to someone

- See the positive side of a negative situation

Create a Better World

Use the creation process to create a better world for yourself and for the people you love. If you are looking at the world today and want to see change, then you need to *be* the change by aligning how you think, feel, speak, and act, accordingly. If you want to create a world of peace then you must feel peaceful and act in a peaceful manner. We sometimes desire something but act very differently because of our emotions. We react to our external environment versus creating our external environment. During the 2016 US presidential election, I saw so many people argue and get angry when debating with friends or family regarding which candidate should win. The debates between friends and colleagues were so heated and passionate. I had friends who told me they would no longer be friends with or talk to people who supported their opposing candidate. It was funny because everyone I knew stood for the same positive values, such as diversity, peace, and inclusion yet their behaviors were completely the opposite. There was no finding a common ground or a desire to understand someone else's point of view. I realized my emotions would get so elevated when I talked politics that I refused to talk about the election. I knew I needed to get to a place where I could approach the conversations with an open mind without letting my negative emotions get in the way. I needed to hear and respect people's point of view and share mine without the expectation of changing someone's mind. I needed to be the change to see the change.

The world is asking us all to wake up and realize the power we have. If you stay in the low vibration negative emotional state then nothing will change for the better. When you are living in fear, you give your power away to someone else. When you raise your vibration, and come from a place of love, you align yourself with the spiritual forces that create everything. Love conquers fear. This is why we admire people like Martin Luther King Jr and Gandhi because they knew this. Your world changes for the better only if you truly shift what is inside you to what you desire. If you shift, your world shifts. That is how your world works.

"We but mirror the world. All the tendencies present in the outer world are to be found in the world of our body. If we could change ourselves, the tendencies in the world would also change. As a man changes his own nature, so does the attitude of the world change towards him. This is the divine mystery supreme."

~Gandhi

(civil rights leader, 1869-1948)

How to Create

1. In order to consciously create anything you desire, the process is always a four- step process. The only difference is the length of time it may take to manifest what you desire.

2. Step 1: Create a clear conscious thought, desire, or intention. Picture your desire in your mind, feel it, and believe it. Build a vision of your desire by using your imagination and receiving inspiration. Focus only on WHAT you desire and don't worry about the HOW.

3. Step 2: Express gratitude as if you have already received it. The feeling of gratitude is a very powerful creative force because it creates an internal vibrational alignment in the Universe with that which you are grateful for.

4. Step 3: Detach from your desire. To create with ease and efficiency, you must detach from your vision. This means you must not feel the feeling of constantly striving for it or wanting it.

5. Step 4: Align your actions with your desire. In this part of the process, you need to trust yourself and the spiritual forces that support you. Depending on your desire, you may not need to take any action. Follow your instincts as to what action is required. Be persistent through obstacles and challenges and know you will achieve your desire.

6. You are at your most powerful when you are in a constant state of non-resistance. When you resist, you create energetic friction and you put up barriers to your life desires. Release resistance through acceptance, forgiveness, and admittance.

7. You have the power to change the world by aligning how you think, feel, speak, and act, according to your positive desires. If you want to create a world of peace then you must feel peaceful and act in a peaceful manner.

Chapter Seven
Everything is a Choice

"We can complain because rose bushes have thorns, or rejoice because thorn bushes have roses."

~Abraham Lincoln
(16th U.S. President, 1809-1865)

The world you live in is made up of infinite possibilities, and in every moment, you are making a choice as to what to think, feel, speak or do. The choices you make are what create your experiences. Therefore, you live in a world of infinite choices. You can create new things in your life by making new choices, and you can experience the same things by making the same choices. It all comes down to taking the time to consciously choose what you want in your life. You are meant to make your own choices and to follow what is in your heart. Life presents you with things you like and things you don't like, or things you perceive as positive or things you perceive as negative. You have the power to choose that which is positive and serves you, and by choosing it, you can create it in your life. The creation process starts with a choice of what you desire to create.

The Dual Nature of Reality

Your reality is a function of your choices because the nature of reality is duality. Everything created from Cosmic Consciousness is dual in nature for the purpose of allowing us to experience who we are. Cosmic Consciousness is the only thing that is singular in nature because it is oneness and the source of everything. From oneness comes duality and, as a result, everything in this world has two sides or opposites from which we are able to choose what side we wish to experience. Everything must have an opposite, otherwise you would not be able to experience that thing. This means you can't have good without bad, up without down, or success without failure. Similarly, if you only ever experienced peace and that was all you knew and existed in the world, you would not know what peace is. It would just be. You would have nothing to compare it to in order to understand what peace is. With the existence of conflict, you understand what peace is. With the existence of sadness, you know what happiness is. With the existence of poverty, you know what wealth is. One cannot exist without the other. This is the nature of our reality.

Human beings are dual in nature. We have good parts of us and bad parts of us. We are both positive and negative. Every atom that makes up our bodies has both a positive charge and a negative charge. We cannot deny our duality as it is part of our nature and part of the world we live in. Without having both positive and negative sides to us we would not be able to recognize and experience positive and negative outside of us. Without the ability to think, feel or act in a dual way, you would not be able to experience and know life. We were created this way for an intelligent reason. Without our dual nature, we could never really know who we truly are. We are both physical and spiritual, seen and unseen, mortal and immortal, limited and unlimited. You cannot experience your true Divine Self without the presence of your mortal self. In a dualistic world, it is the power of choice that creates who you are and the reality you live in. You get to decide what you wish to experience.

"Everything is dual; everything has poles; everything has a pair of opposites; like and unlike are the same; opposites are identical in nature, but different in degree; extremes meet; all truths are but half-truths; all paradoxes may be reconciled."

~The Kybalion
(Hermetic philosophical book)

The Power of Polarity

The dual nature of anything is two sides of the same coin. This means that two polar opposites are connected to each other. From an energetic perspective, polar opposites are the two ends of the same spectrum of energy. For example, love sits on one end of the spectrum of emotion and fear sits on the other end. Similarly, hot sits on one end of the spectrum of temperature and cold sits on the other end. The opposites are the same thing (in this case emotions or temperature), but they just sit at a different point. This applies to all opposites, including challenges and opportunities, lack and abundance, failure and success, and so on. With everything operating on an energetic spectrum, you have the power to choose what side of the spectrum you wish to experience by shifting your internal energy with your thoughts.

"Every explicit duality is an implicit unity."

~Alan Watts
(philosopher, 1915-1973)

The power in understanding the dual nature of everything is the knowledge that contained in everything is the potential for the exact opposite of the same degree or better. What this means is that within everything you perceive as negative is the potential for something positive to the same degree or better. Remember, everything is energy, and you have the ability to harness the energy and transform it into something that serves you. If you are faced with a challenge, know that within the perceived challenge lies the potential for an opportunity, because challenge and opportunity are connected to each other. This is why people say failure breeds success because within failure lies the potential for success. Therefore, when you are experiencing something that feels hard and undesirable, know that this means something good is on the other side of it of equal degree or greater. The challenge is there to help you grow and move you towards your desires. You are meant to wake up and see the challenge as the potential for an opportunity. When you do, you then need to choose to move towards the opportunity with your thoughts. For example, if you experience the pain of a break-up or divorce, know that on the other side of it you will get joy of another relationship that will be better. You need to move through your negative thoughts and feelings with this belief in order to experience something better. Your belief in something better is what will move you towards something better. The potential for the opposite exists, but you need to choose it by believing it will come to you.

I often feel that the Universe needs to send me a loud message for me to wake up and make the change I need to make in my life. These messages always come in ways that can be perceived as negative, stressful, and challenging. One such catalyst for change came in 2009 when I was working for a large retail company in California. I had spent nine years being a dedicated employee and successfully climbing the corporate ladder from the most junior position to mid-level management. I loved working for this company because I loved the work, the people, the culture, the offices, the convenience, and so on. While, I knew I eventually desired to move back to the East Coast to be closer to family, I could not see myself moving anytime soon given how well everything seemed to be going for me. This all changed, however, in what seemed to be an instant when I unconsciously offended the CEO of the holding company while we were both attending a business conference.

While at the conference, the CEO and I had only a few opportunities to interact. The moment of truth for me was during our last interaction when he asked to be my mentor, hoping I would be flattered and see it as a great opportunity to learn and grow in the company. I suppose most everyone would have jumped at the chance but, instead, I saw it as strange given my level within the organization compared with his. More importantly, I was always strongly bothered by his egocentric leadership style, so subconsciously I did not want to learn from someone who leads with values that differed from mine. As a result, when I was confronted with his request, I answered in a jokingly sarcastic way that basically alluded to me saying no without saying no. The words came out of my mouth automatically and uncontrollably. After I responded, I saw by the look on his face that he did not like my answer at all, but I did not anticipate what was going to follow.

After several months passed, I eventually learned how angry he was at me, and how essentially my career was not going to continue to progress as I had hoped unless, somehow, I could turn things around. I was devastated at the knowledge that my nine years of being a valuable and dedicated employee could be thrown completely upside down because of one person who didn't like my response to his question. This felt like an immediate end of my career progression at this company. I even went through the five emotional stages of grief – denial, anger, bargaining, depression, and acceptance. After the denial stage, I immediately knew this was too big to not mean something. I realized I needed this disruptive situation to happen in order for me to get serious about moving my family back East. In fact, I unconsciously created it because I was getting too comfortable where I was, and I needed a reason to leave. I believed that this situation was my catalyst for positive change that was going to lead me to where I was meant to go. As difficult as the situation was for me, I decided to see it as something positive and I knew that this meant something much better was on the other side of it. I also knew that while I was still at the company, I needed to think, feel, and act positively in order to energetically support my positive desires. Within a year, I left the company for a promotion and within two years I moved to the East Coast for an even bigger promotion.

Even when I moved to the East Coast, things did not run as smoothly as I hoped. I continued to face challenges that only made me stronger in my ability to create what I desired in my life. For instance, when I first moved I needed to sell my condo in San Francisco in order to afford to buy a home in New Jersey. I thought selling my condo would be easy and would take less than two months given the hot real estate market in San Francisco at the time. In the meantime, I put all my things in storage and rented a small furnished apartment to live in with my family temporarily. The apartment was too small for the four of us, but it was affordable and I knew we would manage for a few months. Unfortunately, selling my condo did not go as smoothly as I presumed. My real estate agent struggled to find a buyer and it took thirteen months to sell. These thirteen months of uncertainty were very stressful because I felt a huge responsibility to create comfort and stability for my family. We were living in cramped quarters that no one liked for over a year, and we didn't know when we would move. During this challenging time, I knew deep down this was happening to me for a reason. I believed that on the other side of this situation was something wonderful. I even half joked with my husband that the longer it took to sell our condo, the bigger the house we would end up buying. When we finally sold our condo, we closed on the perfect home a few months later. It was everything we said we wanted but better and, yes, bigger than we had imagined. If our condo had sold immediately, we would not have the beautiful home we have today.

You have the ability to transform a negative experience into something positive and wonderful by the energy of your thoughts, feelings, and beliefs. When you experience a hardship, such as a loss of a love, a loss of a job, financial troubles, or business challenges, a lot of negative emotion and energy is created around the situation. In these situations, you feel a higher level of emotion than when things seem to be running smoothly. Many times, your thoughts and emotions go into overdrive because you continue to focus on your troubles. The feelings of anger, frustration, sadness, or fear build energy within you that can either continue to create problems or can be transformed to create something positive that you desire. The energy you build within yourself from your loss can be transformed into energy that creates your gain. The bigger you perceive the negative circumstance, the bigger the potential for something positive. The key is to shift your thinking from what you lost to what you will gain. Even if you do not know what you will gain or how you will gain it, you need to shift out of the negative and move into the possibility of something good. The harder it may seem to do this, the greater the rewards, because that is the secret power of polarity, and how the spiritual world works. Every challenge presents you with the opportunity for something you desire, because challenges and opportunities are energetically linked. You can choose to stay down and suffer, or you can choose to believe that at the other end lies something much better. Remember, the focus of your thoughts creates your reality.

> *"At any moment you have a choice that either leads you closer to your spirit or further away from it."*
> ~Thich Nhat Hanh
> (Monk)

Choose What You Desire

In a world full of infinite choices, you are meant to choose what you truly desire. Through your experiences, you learn what you want and what you don't want. You need to consciously make a choice to experience more of what you want. Make the choice to be who you want to be, do what you want to do, have what you want to have, or experience what you want to experience. You need to make the decision for yourself and not allow anyone else to make it for you. Make the choice with the belief that it is already yours. You will find that some choices manifest easily and some take more time, but regardless of time, your choices will always determine your reality. Therefore, decide what you want and be determined and committed to your desire, especially if it takes more time to manifest.

"The only person you are destined to become is the person you decide to be."

~Ralph Waldo Emerson
(American essayist, 1803-1882)

Sometimes, it is hard for people to understand that everything is a choice because they have created a belief that they do not have a choice in certain aspects of their lives. The truth is, you can always make a different choice. If your choice is made with belief and commitment then it will manifest. Therefore, take the time to decide what you want in all aspects of your life. Choose to have what you desire, and follow the creation process described in the prior chapter to bring it to your reality. The incredible thing about the spiritual and energetic principles behind polarity is your ability to shift where you direct your creative energy from what you do not want to what you want. You have the power to shift where your creative energy flows by shifting where you focus your thoughts. Focus your thoughts on what you desire and decide that it is yours.

Choose the Positive

There is a positive and negative side to everything and everyone. What you choose to see will always be your experience. Therefore, always choose to see the positive side of things. Even when things are challenging, know that something positive will come from it. Because we live in a world of duality, there will always be two sides to everything. Because everything is energy, there will always be positive energy and negative energy. The key is to live in energetic balance or in harmony. If you are experiencing more undesirable situations than desirable situations then you know you are out of balance. If you feel more unease than ease, then you know you are out of balance. The easiest way to keep yourself in balance is to choose to focus on the positive in any negative situation. By focusing on something positive you are shifting your energy to something positive and giving more creative power to the positive. Some strategies to help you choose the positive are as follows:

- See the positive in others: If you are experiencing a negative situation with someone, think of a time when they did something positive for you. By choosing to see something positive in that person you will eliminate any anger or resentment towards them.

- Shift your thoughts to something else completely: If the situation seems too difficult, shift your thoughts to something completely different that still supports you and makes you feel good. For example, if your work situation is frustrating, focus your positive attention on your family or on a personal project.

- Find something to be grateful for: Use the power of gratitude to re-balance your energy and put you in a positive and more focused state of being.

- Imagine the positive that can result from your challenging situation: Use your imagination to create positive scenarios that can come from your negative circumstance. Remember that everything has an opposite, so imagine what this opposite can be.

- Find the lesson you need to learn: See every

challenging situation as something meant for growth. You are meant to learn and grow from all your negative situations. Find what it is you are meant to learn – whether it is a new perspective, a new behavior or quality.

Everything Is a Choice

1. You live in a world of infinite choices, and the choices you make determine your reality.

2. Life presents you with things you like and things you don't like, or things you perceive as positive or things that are negative. You have the power to choose that which is positive and serves you, and by choosing it, you can create it in your life.

3. Everything created from Cosmic Consciousness is dual in nature for the purpose of allowing us to experience who we are. Everything in this world has two sides or opposites from which we are able to choose what side we wish to experience.

4. The power in understanding the dual nature of everything is the knowledge that contained in everything is the potential for the exact opposite of the same degree or better. This means that within anything negative is the potential for something positive to the same degree or better.

5. You have the ability to transform a negative experience to something positive and wonderful by the energy of your thoughts, feelings, and beliefs. If you choose to see a negative situation as the opportunity to something positive, then you will create something positive of equal or greater degree.

6. In a world full of infinite choices, you are meant to choose what you truly desire. Make the choice to be who you want to be, do what you want to do, have what you want to have, or experience what you want to experience.

7. There is a positive and negative side to everything and everyone. What you choose to see will always be your experience. Therefore, always choose to see the positive side of things.

Chapter Eight

Choose Your Story

"Change your story, change your life. Divorce the story of limitation, and marry the story of the truth and everything changes."

~Tony Robbins
(author and businessman)

Everyone loves a good story, whether it is a good movie, book, television show, or a Broadway show. Stories capture our attention, stimulate our minds, teach us something new, and cause us to feel emotion. Most of the time, we think of stories as other people's stories. For example, when you read an engrossing book or watch an entertaining movie, you are lost in someone else's story. You feel how the characters feel and you feel connected and curious about the story being told. For that period of time, you are lost in another world and escape the realities of your world. Other people's stories can make you laugh, make you cry, make you feel every emotion in between, cause you to think differently, or influence your behaviors differently. There is no denying that there is power in storytelling. Even companies and corporate leaders use the power of storytelling to increase customer and employee engagement by connecting with people on an emotional level. The important thing to understand is that the power in a story is not rational nor physical, but it is energetic and spiritual, because stories influence or reflect our thoughts, beliefs, and emotions. Stories have the ability to harness your spiritual energy in a powerful way to keep you in the story. This is why you can easily binge watch your favorite shows on Netflix for hours at a time. Stories have the power to suck you in and keep you there until the story is over or until you decide you no longer like the story.

Other people's stories, or stories that are external to us, have the wonderful purpose of entertaining, inspiring, informing, or educating. Personal stories, on the other hand, have a much greater purpose and power. Personal stories have the power to create your reality because they harness the energy of your thoughts, feelings, and beliefs. Therefore, the most powerful use of storytelling is telling stories about your own life. All of your experiences in the past and present are your stories. These are the stories you need to pay attention to because your personal stories are your reality. If you are looking to change something in your life and in the world around you, then spend less time focusing on other people's stories and more time creating and shaping your own. Your stories are your perspectives on how you view your experiences, and your perspectives create your reality. If you change your perspective, you can change your reality. As a spiritual and creative being, what you experience in your present is a direct reflection of the stories you tell yourself, because your stories are your thoughts, feelings, and beliefs. You have the power to change your past, present, and future by changing your stories and how you tell them. Storytelling is a powerful tool that, if used correctly, can create your supportive positive desires. Correct use of personal story telling are stories that are told in a positive way, support who you truly are, support what you desire in your reality, and help you grow.

Change Your Story

Your stories are your perspectives and your perspectives are not facts or truths unless you believe them to be. Every story can be seen from another perspective; therefore, it is always up to you to decide what perspective you want to see. In general, perspectives can either be positive or negative. Stories you tell that are positive create positive energy and more positive experiences, and the opposite is true for negative stories. Therefore, if you change a negative experience or story to something positive, you create positive energy and create a new positive reality for yourself.

Here is a simple example to illustrate my point. When I went to Portugal with my husband on his business trip, I was spending my days on tours and meeting new people while he was at a conference working. On the last day of our trip I took a food and wine tour of the city. I was with nine other people from different countries. It was a great group of people and we all got along really well. By the end of the two and a half-hour tour I became friendly with three people from the tour and we decided to meet up later that night after dinner. I was on a high from meeting such fun people and I was excited to have my husband meet them later. When I returned to the hotel, my husband was tired from the conference and was not in the mood to stay out late with a group of people. He wanted to have a quiet dinner with just the two of us and then get an early night's sleep because we were flying out early the next morning. While I was looking for more excitement on our last night, I agreed to do what he wanted. After a couple of hours out with my husband, I received a text from one of my new friends asking to meet up at a bar. By then, my husband agreed to meet them since he could tell I really wanted to.

We spent the rest of the night up until 4 a.m. going to many bars and restaurants, and meeting many new people. After only three hours of sleep, I woke up to an angry husband who blamed me for the loss of his very expensive jacket during our night out on the town. We were both very tired and needed to get to the airport. We were barely talking to each other. Based on the words that had been exchanged, everything was going downhill. His mood was worsening. He went from being angry about the loss of his jacket, to telling himself the whole trip was a disaster. I began feeling angry and even guilty, but I was determined for our trip not to be remembered in this way. At the airport, I did whatever I could do to change all my sad and guilty feelings to something more positive. When my husband and I finally spoke, I told him that we needed to change the story. We could see the last night as a disaster or we could see it as one of the best nights we have had recently. I told him to see the evening as evidence that we can still hang out until 4 a.m. with people half our age and have a great time, and that even though he lost his jacket, he could get another one. I was trying to focus on the positive aspects of our night and our trip. When I listened to myself tell this story my feelings of guilt and anger went away. I noticed his anger went away too. When we got home, the night out in Portugal and the lost jacket became a funny story to tell and was no longer a story of anger and blame.

While this story may seem simple, if my husband and I did not change our perspective on the night, our negative feelings of anger and guilt would have persisted, creating more strain on our relationship. By changing our story, we stopped our negative feelings towards each other fairly quickly and came together in a more positive way, which made us both feel better. Another part of our original story of anger and blame was the fact that in the old story my husband saw the loss of his jacket as evidence he was not worthy of the expensive jacket. This was his inner story he was telling himself and me. This is an example of how our stories can hurt us unless we change them. The fact he was not feeling worthy of the expensive jacket created the experience of loss of that jacket. However, you can let the experience validate your belief and inner feelings or you can decide to choose another story. By choosing another story, you start to experience something new, something that makes you feel good. You begin to believe something new. For me and my husband, the story changed from a lack of worth and loss to a funny story about a fun night out. Choose the story you want to live. All it takes is a new perspective.

The stories you tell yourself are creative because they reflect your thoughts, feelings, and beliefs. You have the power to change them because you are in control of them. You will not change the actual events but you will change your perception of the events. Your perception will change how you feel and think about the events. As your feelings change from negative to neutral or positive, you put your inner being in alignment to create new positive experiences. Remember, everything is energy, and in the spiritual realm we communicate and create with our energy. We also live in a dual reality in which everything has two sides. Therefore, choose a new story for yourself that is positive and supportive, keep telling yourself the new story until it becomes your true story, then experience how your world shifts for the better. Use the below guidance to practice what it feels like to change a story from negative to positive.

- Identify a story in your past in which you felt like you were wronged or a victim.

- Write the story down and read it out loud.

- Notice how the story makes you feel.

- Now, change the story and tell it from the hero's point of view. Find an aspect of the story that you can make into something positive.

- Write it down and read it out loud.

- Notice how the story makes you feel – if you successfully changed your story, then your feelings will shift from negative to positive.

What stories do you tell yourself that don't help or support you? Do you tell yourself you are not worthy? Do you tell yourself you are not meant to experience a loving relationship, you are not creative, you are not a good manager of money, you can't handle working and raising a family, you aren't meant to experience the luxuries of life? If you keep experiencing the same unwanted situations over and over again, or you want to experience something new, then a story about yourself needs to change. For example, I have a friend who has told me many times that she would send a gift to someone she knows and would never receive a response or a thank you from them. The beautiful thing about my friend is that she is very thoughtful and caring when she picks something out for someone. Oftentimes, she would send a gift without there being a specific occasion. Initially, I was confused and even upset when she told me she never received an acknowledgment. It was not until she told me her story that I understood what was going on. My friend had a story of not being worthy enough. She craved acceptance and feared rejection. Her actions (sending gifts) were done with the intention of wanting acceptance. What she was experiencing was how she was feeling, not what she was desiring. Old patterns do not change until you change your story, but in order to do so you first need to identify your negative story like my friend was able to do. Take the time to think of one or two most harmful stories you tell yourself. Then follow the below exercise to change it into something positive.

- Make a short list of the negative stories you tell yourself (one to three stories).

- Next to each point on your list, change the negative to a positive – for example: "I am not worthy of having anything expensive," changes to, "I deserve the best this life has to offer."

- Create a story for yourself that supports your positive statement – see your story in your mind and feel your new story.

- Read your positive statements and stories over and over again until they become your new stories.

Create Your Story

You have the power to create the story you want to live. Once you create your story, you need to live into your story. My nine-year old daughter, Samar, exemplifies the power of living her story in her beautiful child-like innocent way. On her eighth birthday at school, Samar was asked by her teacher to choose someone in her class to help her pass out treats. After Samar made her choice, one of her friends, Stella (name changed), was upset she had not been chosen. Stella decided that because she was not chosen, she would not talk to or play with Samar anymore. It became clear to Samar that her friendship with Stella was not the same. While Samar was hurt and confused by the situation, she refused to let it get her down. She could have easily been the victim, but instead she decided to live what she wished to experience. Every day Samar would make the effort to be nice to Stella even if Stella was not being friendly to her. Samar continued to act like they were still friends even through situations where she was rejected or ignored. Within a few weeks, Stella finally came around and they were friends again. Samar consciously chose a happy ending and she got one. While this may seem like a simple children's situation, it was a very powerful story when she told it to me. I saw how she made a conscious choice to live into the story she wanted. Even after she was rejected time and time again, she stayed positive, determined to create a different outcome. While living her story was not easy, she knew the only way to get the outcome she desired was to act like she already had what she desired. Samar is very wise. She reminded me that you can create the story you want to live, but you need to live into that story. You need to believe it, feel it, and act as if it is already your story. This is the power of conscious creation.

Create a story that is unique to you. Even if no one else you know is living that story, when you believe your story and live your story, your experiences will start to support your story. Create your life story based on what you want for yourself, not what other people want for you or what others are doing. When I first had kids, everyone told me my life would change and I would have to change who I was. Based on what I saw around me, changing who I was meant sacrificing my personal desires, spending my time shuttling kids around to sports and activities, and being weighed down by the responsibility of having a child. While I knew my life would change, I wanted to create a new life that I desired and not what other people were experiencing. I wanted to have it all – be a good mother, enjoy my career, and enjoy my life. I decided to follow the strategy that if Mommy is happy then the kids will be happy.

As a result, when I had my children, I integrated them into my life. I balanced their needs and my desires. I was determined to be the happiest mother; therefore, I always spoke positively about my new experiences as a mother and never complained even though I was frequently operating on lack of sleep. I tried to stay relaxed around my kids and refused to stress out if they did not eat a meal or fall asleep at a particular time. My husband and I continued to do the things we loved to do on the weekends, but now together with our kids. From a very early age our kids got used to our lifestyle of eating out, traveling, and skiing. Childcare worked out easily, which supported my desire to continue to work without feeling concerned about the welfare of my children. In fact, having children helped me to create a more balanced and productive work life. My children enhanced my life and did not change my life. In fact, as my children grow older, my life is even more joyful and fulfilling because that is the story I choose to live. When you create your unique story, you need to live your story in what you think, believe, say, and act. By living into your story, you will find the universal creative energy of Cosmic Consciousness will support you and bring into your life that which supports your new story.

Tell Your Story

There are stories we all have that we are afraid to tell other people. These are the stories that we are embarrassed by, or which make us feel bad, or ashamed. These stories are our secrets and by not telling them we think they will go away. However, the truth is, these stories that we hide from are our more interesting stories. If you harness the negative energy these stories create in you and release the energy, you remove energetic barriers that hold you back from creating more of what you desire. There is a lot of creative energetic power in the stories you hide. Therefore, be brave and tell your story. By doing so, you make yourself lighter and open yourself up energetically to receive more good in your life. Plus, your story will most likely be a way to inspire others or help people through their own hidden stories.

After the birth of my second child, I experienced an aggressive form of alopecia – an autoimmune disorder that results in the loss of hair. The experience of losing all my hair was terrifying. I had lived with alopecia all my life, but it was always manageable and unnoticeable before. This time, the loss was more severe and I was not responding to my usual treatments of cortisone injections. I tried different solutions, such as topical creams, acupuncture, and special shampoos, but nothing worked. Week after week, month after month, my hair did not stop falling out and I began to feel stressed and depressed. I dreaded showering every day because the hair I would lose in the shower was a constant reminder that I was going bald. I had spent several months feeling scared, insecure, and self-conscious, but I was determined to look and feel like my old self again. After many months of searching for a solution, I found a woman who specialized in hair loss and extensions. She understood what I was going through and she helped me through my hair loss. I quickly went from hair extensions to wearing a full wig and fake eyelashes, as the hair loss accelerated and I lost all of my hair. Throughout this experience, I was determined to hide what was happening to me from my colleagues, my friends, most of my family, and even my children. The only people I initially confided in were my husband and my parents. I did not want people to look at me differently or see me as not being good enough. I was determined to hide what I considered to be a personal flaw or weakness. I was successful at keeping my secret because my wig looked so natural. Even my dermatologist was surprised when I told her I was wearing a wig.

It wasn't until I was at a leadership retreat with colleagues from work three years later, that I summoned the courage to tell my story. At part of this retreat, each one of us had the opportunity to share our personal stories that had shaped us as people and leaders. I watched how my colleagues who spoke before me were so honest, trusting, and vulnerable in their story telling. I knew this was the time that I needed to be honest and share my story with them. When it was my turn to tell my life story, I was shaking and emotional because I was about to reveal the fact I was wearing a wig. I had consciously hidden this secret for so long that when I finally expressed the truth and told my story I released a lot of tears. Even though everyone was very supportive and respectful, I initially regretted telling my story wondering if it was worth the embarrassment. Regardless, I had finally told my secret to colleagues and so I knew it was also time to share it with others who were close to me. When I came home, I finally told my young children who reacted with such innocent curiosity yet I knew it did not change how they saw me. I slowly started to tell more friends and family who responded in the same way. The more people I told, the lighter I felt. The negative energy I released by telling my story opened me up to receive more positive things in my life, including new relationships and deeper relationships with people. Over the next two years, I started to share my story more confidently as it no longer had a negative emotional hold over me. By telling your story, you start to own your story instead of your story owning you. Spiritually, this means you take your creative power back by releasing the negative energy that imprisons you. When you take your creative power back, you become a more powerful conscious creator.

Choose Your Story

1. Stories have power. The power in a story is not rational nor physical; instead, it is energetic and spiritual because stories influence or reflect our thoughts, beliefs, and emotions.

2. Your stories are your perspectives on how you view your experiences, and your perspectives create your reality. Change your perception of your experience and you can change your story.

3. If you change a negative experience or story to something positive, you create positive energy and create a new positive reality for yourself.

4. You have the power to create the story you want to live. Once you create your story, you need to live into your story in how you think, what you say, and how you act in order to manifest it into your reality.

5. Tell your hidden stories. By releasing the negative energy these stories create in you, you remove energetic barriers that hold you back from creating more of what you desire.

Chapter Nine

Question Reality

"You are not IN the Universe, you ARE the Universe, an intrinsic part of it. Ultimately, you are not a person, but a focal point where the universe is becoming conscious of itself."

~Eckhart Tolle
(spiritual author)

I always thought I was spiritual, but I held spirituality separate from my physical life. I thought quotes like "be the change you want to see in the world" or "you already have everything you need" were idealistic and did not relate to my physical reality. For years, I shied away from reading and studying spiritual teachings because I thought I would be encouraged to give up the material possessions or experiences I enjoyed. However, the deeper I looked for answers as to how to improve my physical reality or strategies to achieve my goals, the answers lay in spirituality. The source of all my experiences come from the spiritual realm. Spirituality is an awareness of the existence of the unseen, all-powerful, all-encompassing, all-knowing, all-loving Cosmic Consciousness or God. I realized spirituality and physicality are directly connected and not separate. The spiritual world creates the physical world; therefore, there is no separation. I no longer needed to fear that focusing more on the spiritual would discourage my worldly desires. It is the understanding of who we are spiritually that allows us to fulfill our deepest desires in this world. It is an understanding that our spiritual powers are our true creative powers. Therefore, it is the inward focus that directs the outward actions in order to achieve desires in the easiest way.

Unfortunately, most of us live our lives reacting to the external and acting based on reactionary thoughts and feelings. We do this because we were never taught that our power lies in our ability to create, and we give up our power when we automatically react based on non-supportive conditioned beliefs and emotions. For example, it is like getting an email from someone who is expressing aggression or frustration towards you. You may automatically feel anger after reading that email and immediately send an email back in the same tone. The back and forth may continue for a while until finally you both talk in person and then you both calm down. This is action based on reaction. I find this to be the longer and harder route to achieving anything. Life becomes more fun when you stop reacting and you start creating, and creation can only happen if you directly interact with the unseen realm first and go within yourself. When I get emails that trigger a negative emotion, such as frustration or anger, I no longer respond right away. I notice how I am feeling and I wait until I am fully in control of my own feelings and thoughts before I respond. Oftentimes, my response will include a request to discuss the issue in person which gives me more time to relax and focus my thoughts towards what I desire to create. By taking control of my own feelings and re-focusing my thoughts on my desired positive outcome, I harness my own power to create with ease. Your world and your Universe is within you despite what you observe outside of you. It is your consciousness that is connected to all of consciousness. Therefore, in order to impact anything, you need to first go to the energetic source that lies within you.

The Physical World Is Not Solid

Reality is not what it seems to be. It is so much more interesting, magical, and malleable than what most of us think. In fact, the physical world is not really physical at its deepest level. Everything in the Universe is energy and vibrates at its own frequency. Science, through quantum physics, has proven this to be true. Every atom is made up of vortexes of energy that constantly vibrate. Scientists have observed that the closer you look at an atom and its structural make up, you notice that it is mainly empty space. Atoms are not physical at all because atoms are pure energy. The construct of everything is, therefore, energy. The only difference between what we see physically and what is unseen or un-manifest is the rate of energetic vibration. Physical matter is energy vibrating at a very slow rate, and the un-manifest is energy vibrating at a very high rate.

> *"If you want to know the secrets of the Universe, you need to think in terms of energy, frequency, and vibration."*
> ~**Nikola Tesla**
> **(inventor, 1856-1943)**

By opening yourself up to the energetic nature of everything, you will understand you are connected to everything at this energetic level. The universal language is vibration and frequency. This is the most powerful and important language to learn if you truly want to become the master manifestor of your life. You create in your reality by sending out vibrational frequencies that attract like vibrational frequencies. Your thoughts, feelings, beliefs, and words are the energetic means by which we interact and create in the Universe. You become a powerful creator when you can consciously harness your own energy and direct it into what you desire.

> *"Everything is energy and that is all there is to it. Match the frequency of the reality you want and you cannot help but get that reality. It can be no other way. This is not philosophy. This is physics."*
>
> **~Albert Einstein**
> **(theoretical physicist, 1879-1955)**

Through quantum physics, scientists have observed that the observer creates the reality. Science is starting to prove that reality is created from within, which is what spiritual teachers have been communicating for thousands of years. The quantum double split experiment is the most well-known experiment in which the observer produces the results of the measurements. In this experiment, researchers observed that a beam of electrons is effected by the act of being observed. It was observed that the greater amount of observation, the greater the influence on what was taking place. The experiment showed that the beam of electrons act like both a wave and particles. When acting like a wave, the particles can pass through several openings (or the double slit) in a barrier and come together at the other end. The interesting thing was that when electrons were being observed, they acted like particles versus waves. If they were observed to go through one slit, then it was clear they did not go through the other slit. It was only

when the electrons were not observed that they went
through both slits and acted like waves.

There have been several other finds in the field of
quantum physics which have suggested that consciousness
creates reality, and everything is connected on an energetic
level. However, you don't need to rely on scientific
experiments to prove what you can observe for yourself.
By changing your perspective on the connected nature of
the world, and by stretching your mind to see who you
are in relation to your world, you can observe how you
can change your world. Your consciousness is directly
connected to the Universe through a connected energetic
field of Cosmic Consciousness. Your perspectives are what
shape and mold what you observe and experience. The
world you live in is an energy field that bends and molds
based on your intentions, desires, and behaviors.

> *"Everything emerges and returns to a fundamental field of
> information that connects us all."*
>
> ~**Nassim Haramein**
> (physicist)

Is Reality An Illusion?

Some people liken the reality we live in to a matrix or
a computer program. I am not saying this is true or false,
but it is an interesting way to think about the world we live
in and how we interact with it. Similar to the movie *The
Matrix,* this would mean whatever we perceive is not true
reality, and instead, it is just an experience. What is real
is what is beyond the program, and we haven't yet woken
up from the program. This concept of reality is similar
to when you dream at night. Most of the time when you

dream at night, you are in a dream but not aware that it is a dream. You are able to think and feel when you are dreaming, and have an experience, though the experience is usually hazy. Your dreams are creations that come from your mind. Your dreams are created by your innermost thoughts and emotions. When you wake up, you realize it was just a dream. However, if you have ever realized in your dream that you are in a dream, you will know you can control your dream with your conscious thoughts and you have the power to do and create anything you want. If you decide you want to fly, you will fly in your dream. This is called lucid dreaming. Similarly, in your waking life, if you realize you are in a program or a dream, you have the ability to influence your experiences in the same way, through your conscious thoughts. However, unlike lucid dreaming where the results are instantaneous, it takes more internal effort, alignment, and time in this state of reality. Additionally, if you have done any research on Near Death Experiences or heard stories from people who have had them, the common experience of those who have entered the spiritual realm for a period of time is that in the higher realm every thought and desire manifests immediately. This is the nature of who we are – creating with our thoughts.

Let's expand on the program idea a little further. Think of this reality as a computer program similar to a virtual reality simulation. Think of your body as your virtual reality head gear. You are able to perceive your reality through your body by decoding the program from your brain. Your brain is the computer. The computer code is what allows you to see everything as separate and in physical form. Your five senses are used to perceive what you consider reality. These senses are electrical signals that are registered in the brain. The only reason why a table is solid is because your brain decodes it as solid based on the electrical signals of touch. Your thoughts and emotions also send electrical signals to your brain and your brain decodes your reality accordingly.

Once, when I was at a restaurant, I observed my appetizer being brought to me by my waiter. I saw that the food itself was placed in some sort of decorative stone. For some reason, in my mind I thought it was a hot stone. When the waiter set the appetizer down, I touched the stone and automatically felt it was burning hot, so I quickly pulled my finger away while shrieking, "Ouch!" A few days later, when my husband and I were discussing our meal at the restaurant, I realized the stone had actually been ice cold. He ordered the same appetizer and looked at me strangely and corrected me when I said I felt the opposite. Did my thoughts and feelings impact the program? Similarly, have you ever experienced watching something violent on TV and felt slight pain in your own body? This is when the electrical signals from your thoughts and emotions get decoded as a physical feeling purely based on something inside of you – not what is real. It is what is inside the body that is experienced outside the body.

This computer program concept and similar concepts are meant to illustrate the nature of how our worlds work. The reality is, there is no separation between you and your reality. Science, philosophy, and spirituality are converging on these same ideas. As new discoveries are made, more questions are asked. We will never know the answer to everything, but what we do know now can dramatically change the way we live.

"Reality is merely an illusion, albeit a very persistent one."
~Albert Einstein (theoretical physicist, 1879-1955)

Why Are You Here?

If this world isn't as real as we think it is, then what is it all about? The reason why you are here is to discover who you really are. You are not just your mind, body, and personality, or the ego-self. There is another part of you, your spiritual-self, that is connected to everything and is a part of Cosmic Consciousness. You are a Divine Creator, here to finally realize your true nature. You are here to create and experience something that is unique to you. The part of you that speaks to you through your heart, is the soul and the spiritual part of you. This is the part of you that you feel that pushes through your chest. It knows what it came here to experience and it is up to you to listen and hear what it is telling you. Often, we ignore this inner voice. The routine of our daily lives and our external conditioning keeps this inner voice tucked away. The part of you that pushes away the inner voice is your ego-self because the ego will never make it easy for you to listen to your soul-self. Without acknowledging the soul-self that lives within you, you can never find your true self. By listening to and following your soul-self, you will experience the fullest expression of who you really are.

Your soul-self is that part of you that knows what you truly love because it *is* love. If you follow what you love, then you will have the power of all Cosmic Consciousness supporting you, if you trust it. If you don't know yet what you love or what your purpose is, your job is to do what you can to figure it out. Living on purpose is what you are meant to do. This is what will give you the happiness and fulfillment you are looking for. If you are not satisfied with where you are in life and you know you need to do something else but you don't know what it is, this is your soul-self calling out to you. This desire for something else is your soul-self pushing you to wake up to who you are and what you are meant to do in this world. Keep searching until you find it, because that is why you are here.

Your personal search for your purpose has to start internally first. In meditation, when you quiet the chatter of your mind, you can connect to Cosmic Consciousness and the soul part of you. If you have never meditated before, it will take some time and practice, but the benefits will be worth it. When you go into meditation, ask the Universe and your innermost being what you are longing to know. Ask it sincerely with a sense of detachment to how the answer will come. You might hear your inner voice talking to you or you might receive answers later in the day as you interact in the physical world (through other people, songs, written messages, and so on). You might be drawn to a mentor or to travel. Whatever it is, follow those callings and instincts because they are coming from your soul-self. If you truly desire to know your purpose, you will be guided to your answer. Anything you truly desire with your heart will come to you with the conscious effort of thinking, feeling, and believing, which will then guide your actions.

Once you know your purpose, you need to decide to live your purpose. Everything is a choice. You can choose to stay where you are or you can choose to live your purpose. When you make a choice, commit to it. You can and are supposed to create this experience in your life. However, most people do not, because they do not understand the natural and Divine powers that they already possess. They do not know how to correctly use the tools they were given. Negative thoughts, feelings, and beliefs limit people from being who they are truly meant to be.

Put your ego in check and find the voice of your soul-self.

Your spiritual-self has no fear and no limitation. This is the part of you that has all the power. The ego-self ultimately fears death and encourages your thoughts to be fear based. The fear that exists inside of you when you consider doing something different or pushing yourself out of your comfort zone is from your ego-self. The fears are only false fears when you understand that you create your reality. You may fear financial loss, loss of a job, loss of a loved one, loss of security, and so on. These are false beliefs when you realize how reality truly works. The ego-self also looks for approval and acceptance outside of itself. The soul-self does not need to look outside itself because it knows it is connected to the creative forces that create everything. It is one with everything and it is eternal. The next time you go looking for approval from someone or look for someone to make you feel better about yourself because you are feeling insecure, don't do it. Force yourself to do nothing. Instead, stop and center yourself. As hard as it may feel, you have the power to eliminate all your feelings of fear or insecurity yourself. Meditate and clear your thoughts. Bring yourself to a place of calmness and balance. Do not think into the situation that made you feel this way. This is the quickest way to change your circumstance. Your inner being creates your outer experiences always. You will then find your external experiences will support your new inner feelings.

******

By questioning reality, you open yourself up to find your own truth, putting you in the realm of all possibility. Only you will know your truth by your own exploration. By questioning who you are and how the world works, you start to get answers that you are more than what you think you are. You are more capable and powerful than you think. Your reality becomes a much more interesting experience, because you expand your boundaries of knowledge. By expanding your mind, you expand your experiences. Humanity evolves because we are constantly seeking knowledge. As we learn new things, we create new things, and we continue to progress. We know more today, as a species, than we knew one hundred years ago. We will know a lot more still in the next ten years. As technology advances and the information flow increases, humanity will progress at a much faster rate. Be open to new information and you might find the right idea, notion, piece of wisdom, or practice that changes your life.

Question Reality

1. The physical world is not really physical at its deepest level. Scientists have observed that the closer you look at an atom and its structural make-up, you will notice that it is mainly empty space.

2. Everything in the Universe is energy and vibrates at its own frequency. The only difference between what we see physically and what is unseen or un-manifest is the rate of energetic vibration.

3. Your consciousness is directly connected to the Universe through a connected energetic field of Cosmic Consciousness. Your perspectives are what shape and mold what you observe and experience.

4. You are here in this reality to discover and experience who you really are. You are meant to listen to your inner voice and follow your heart.

5. By questioning who you are and how the world works, you will start to get answers that you are more than what you think you are.

Chapter Ten

Test Your Power

"If you want to awaken all of humanity, then awaken all of yourself. If you want to eliminate the suffering in the world, then eliminate all that is dark and negative in yourself. Truly, the greatest gift you have to give is that of your own self-transformation."

~Lao Tzu
(Chinese philosopher, 6th-5th century BC)

The only way for you to truly discover and believe in who you are and the Divine powers that you have is to test it for yourself. You will discover what is true for you based on your own experiences. However, like anything new, learning how to do something takes practice and discipline. To get good at something takes real commitment. It is similar to learning to be good at a sport or learning to play an instrument. It takes time and practice to consistently create, but once you see the benefits, you will be encouraged to continue to practice. Eventually, it will become a new part of how you operate in the world and you will start to really enjoy life.

If you are committed to making a change in your life, then you are willing to do what it takes to achieve your goals. Most people think to achieve anything concrete (a relationship, money, a new job, a healthy body), you need to take some specific physical action. We go straight to what we need to do in the physical world. I operated in this way for practically my whole life and I can truly look back and be proud of what I have accomplished. A lot of what I was taught and was conditioned to believe created wonderful things in my life. At the same time, I realized my old habits and conditioned beliefs were also holding me back from expressing who I really was and what I truly desired. Therefore, I do not judge how we mainly focus on the physical realm, since this is the world we live in and what we have been taught. However, my goal is to show you there is a more direct and efficient way to achieve your goals. If you are going to put in effort, then direct your effort and your energy wisely. Anything that is created in the physical world starts in the spiritual world. Your efforts should always be directed internally first. By spending time building your internal awareness, learning new habits, and practicing the use of your powers, you are accelerating your path to your desires. The more you practice, the more powerful you will become as a conscious creator of your reality.

Practices

Stop thinking: Thinking is your Divine creative power. In order to consciously create, you need to first build awareness of your thoughts and the ability to control your thoughts. Become aware of the fact that your mind is constantly racing when you are not specifically focused on anything. Find those moments when you do not need to use a lot of mental energy (commuting to work, cleaning the house, taking a shower, etc.) and ask yourself:

- What am I thinking right now?

- Are these thoughts serving a purpose that benefits me or are they wasted energy?

Practice becoming aware of what you are thinking. There is no need to go into why you are thinking those thoughts; only to become aware of your thoughts. When you become aware, you stop thinking in that moment. If your racing thoughts are useless then consciously stop thinking those thoughts. Become present in what you are doing in the moment and feel the difference in your mind and body when you are free from your unconscious thoughts. If new thoughts start to come in, remember to become present again by asking the same questions as you did before. This will help to build the muscle of awareness and thought control. The purpose of this practice to is help you get good at not thinking. You can practice this anytime and anywhere. By not thinking unnecessary thoughts, you will conserve more energy, which will make your conscious and directed thoughts more powerful.

Meditate: I found meditation to be hugely beneficial in building my muscle of awareness and thought control. If you have never mediated before, you can start the practice in a very simple way.

- Find a comfortable and quiet place to sit – either in a chair with your feet flat on the ground and your arms resting on your thighs, or by sitting crossed-legged in a lotus position.

- Set your phone alarm for a minimum of ten minutes.

- Close your eyes, relax your body, and focus your attention on breathing.

- When thoughts come into your mind, bring your attention back to your breathing.

- Stay relaxed throughout the process.

- When the alarm sounds then slowly open your eyes.

This meditation practice, if done regularly, will strengthen your ability to quiet your thoughts. When you first try mediation, it might seem difficult to shut off your thoughts, but with practice it gets much easier. Set a daily practice of meditation. I would recommend meditating first thing in the morning before you start the day. When ten minutes becomes easy and enjoyable, then extend your practice to twenty or even thirty minutes.

Build Emotional Awareness: As often as you can, ask yourself how you are feeling. When you are feeling extremely angry (because someone did something to you) or frustrated (road rage when driving somewhere), try to catch yourself and ask yourself:

- How am I feeling right now?

- Are these feelings helping me?

Ask yourself these questions at any moment of the day. Having to dig a bit deeper to truly understand your feelings in any given moment is hugely beneficial in building emotional awareness. Your emotions are your added energetic powers, which you need to be able to consciously use in the creation process. Awareness and control over your emotions is needed to consciously create. It is those underlying emotions that you are not consciously aware of that build barriers to your desires.

Create Your Day: Before you start your day, set an intention for your day. Clear your mind of all thoughts and state in your mind what kind of day you want to have. You can do this right before you begin your mediation practice. Ask yourself:

- What do I want to accomplish today?

- How do I want to feel?

Once you know what you want to experience and feel during your day, use the process discussed in the chapter, How to Create, to begin the creative process of bringing your desire into your reality.

- Step 1: Set your intention – think it, really feel it in your body, and believe it.

- Step 2: Express gratitude – be grateful as if you already experienced what you desire.

- Step 3: Detach from your intention and the outcome of your day.

- Step 4: Follow through on any actions required in your day that are aligned with your intention.

Spend no more than a couple minutes on steps one through three. Get clear, feel good, be thankful, and then release. If you are in meditation, then spend the rest of the time free of any mental thoughts. Do not keep thinking into your intention. You have to let it go. Consciously setting the intention for the day never fails, if done correctly. Your practice should start out simple, yet it should align with something you desire and believe. Remember, belief is the foundation for creating your reality. Do not attempt to set an intention for yourself that is out of your current belief system. You can start simply by intending a productive and happy day, or by having an intention that you will feel good about yourself today. The goal is for you to practice your creative abilities of bringing into your reality that which you desire. By practicing on simple things, you will begin to build up the confidence and belief to create bigger things in your life.

If you find that you didn't experience your intention for the day, then go back and examine what went wrong in your creation process. It is important for you to become self-aware about what worked for you and what didn't work for you in order to become a master creator. Ask yourself the following questions:

- How were you feeling when you set your intention?

- Did you have any doubt that your intention would manifest?

- Did you really let go of your intention? Did you trust it was coming to you or were you constantly thinking about it during the day?

- Were there any negative thoughts and emotions during your day that created barriers?

It is important that you are honest with yourself when you answer these questions. Once you can identify what went wrong, you can apply your new understanding when creating a new intention for the next day. The important thing is that you do not give up. The creation process works. However, like anything new, you need to practice it in order to understand how the process works best for you. You need to assess what it feels like to you when it works for you and when it does not work.

The practice of consciously creating your day is recommended because it is a quick way to see the results of your creative powers. By experiencing your own creative abilities, you will build a deeper belief and confidence in your Divine powers. Another quick way to see the results of your creative abilities is to set an intention for a particular event, right before you go out for the evening, right before a meeting, or anything you want to influence. Go through steps one through three before the event. Find a quiet space and think, feel, believe, and release your intention. By creating small things in your life, you will see the results of your creative process quickly. You will learn and adjust quickly. Bigger goals and desires take more time. You need a deeper belief in your powers and patience to manifest the bigger things.

Strengthen Your Personal Power: By strengthening your willpower, you strengthen your power to create. Practice strengthening your will by shifting negative thoughts and emotions to neutral or positive. This is never an easy thing to do, especially when your negative emotions are strong. Therefore, it takes the strength of your will to shift negative emotions into something positive or productive. When you are able to shift from a negative emotion into something that serves you, you will experience the power to create your positive desires. You will experience for yourself your ability to shift the energy of something negative into something positive.

I am not asking you not to feel and acknowledge your negative emotions. You need to feel and acknowledge what you are feeling in order to move through negative emotions effectively. You may not be able to do this immediately each time you notice a negative emotion. Start at whatever level of emotion you can manage. I have found the most fun emotion for me to shift is anxiety. Shifting anxiety to excitement is not a big jump. When I feel anxious, many times I don't know why. If I tell myself it's excitement for something that is going to happen, and I feel myself enter another vibration, I then feel better and know my energy is aligned with my positive desires. Similarly, if you are feeling anxiety and uncomfortable because you are experiencing the unknown, you are in luck! The unknown can either paralyze you and keep you stuck, or it is an opportunity to create something wonderful. The unknown is the realm of all possibility. By staying in negative emotions of low vibration, you stop your ability to create something you desire. When you feel this sense of anxiousness, try hard to shift it to excitement – even just a low feeling of excitement. Feel how it feels and stay in that feeling until you are no longer controlled by your emotions.

Build Your Belief: Overall, you need to believe in yourself and your capabilities. You need to believe that you have the power to create and that the forces of Cosmic Consciousness can consciously work for you as often as you like. Do whatever you can to create that belief in yourself. Read books, do research, go on retreats, travel, talk to people, or practice what you have already learned. Belief is the foundation. Your belief will guide you. If your beliefs are not aligned with your deepest desires, then work on building your belief. Find the tools and strategies that work for you. Use vision boards or mind movies to help you envision in your mind what you desire to create. Use journals to help you identify your desires, limiting beliefs, or to practice the things in your life that you are grateful for. Find the strategies that connect with you and can help you believe what you desire is possible. It's time you know who you are and start to believe in yourself.

Remember, you are here to discover who you are. Push yourself out of your box and see what the Universe creates for you. You have the power to create your world. Everyone has this power, because we are all part of Cosmic Consciousness itself. We are all connected. Be who you are meant to be and you will automatically change your world for the greater good. It is not a hard thing to do unless you think it is hard. Everything starts from the inside first.

Epilogue

Writing this book has been a reminder to myself of the power I have and we all have to create the world we live in. By immersing myself in this content every day throughout the writing process, I found myself becoming much more in tune with my connection to everything, and in awe of the unseen forces that are in us and around us, always there to support us if tuned into correctly. I experienced myself becoming a much stronger creator of my reality because I was consciously applying the disciplines and practices I mentioned in this book every day. At the same time, I have become more consciously aware of my humanness. At times, I still find myself reacting and acting based on strong negative emotions. I try not to beat myself up over it by reminding myself that I am still human. I am dual in nature and I cannot eliminate one part of myself but can only work to evolve, grow, and learn from that part of me. As you begin to discover your inner powers and your ability to create your reality grows stronger, remember your humanness and take it easy on yourself. Life is a journey so try to enjoy it along the way.

I believe my personal growth journey will never end. I continue to be very curious to understand more about who I am and how this world works. I don't think I can ever really know everything, but I do believe I am meant to further pursue this knowledge and share what I know to be beneficial with others. There are many people who are dedicating their lives to helping people wake up to their true empowered and spiritual selves, and I encourage you to learn from as many people as you feel connected to. I feel a strong sense of momentum happening around self-realization which makes it a very exciting time to be alive. We all deserve to know who we really are and become who we are meant to be. It is your right to find your hidden light.

I have included a sample list of books that have inspired me along my journey so far that I hope you find useful. For additional information about me, future projects, and additional resources, please visit *www.yourhiddenlight.com.*

Resources

Listed alphabetically by title:

Autobiography of a Yogi, Paramahansa Yogananda

Change Your Thoughts, Change Your life, Wayne Dyer

Conversations with God Book 1, 2, 3, Neale Donald Walsch

The Impersonal Life, Joseph Benner

Message from the Masters, Brian Weiss

Outwitting the Devil, Napoleon Hill

The Power of Now, Eckhart Tolle

The Secret, Rhonda Byrne

Secrets of the Millionaire Mind, T. Harv Eker

The Seven Spiritual Laws of Success, Deepak Chopra

Think and Grow Rich, Napoleon Hill

Please visit *www.yourhiddenlight.com* for additional resources.

About the Author

Raana Zia has spent her career holding executive level leadership roles in large Fortune 500 retail companies including the position of Chief Financial Officer. She has spent over 15 years developing leaders and coaching people and teams to maximize their abilities and achieve their goals in the corporate world. Her passion for personal and leadership development and an intense desire to discover her own purpose and potential led her down an unexpected path of self-realization and spirituality. Raana's journey into self-discovery opened her up to a greater understanding of her direct connection and influence over her reality. Her realizations and personal experiences compelled her to write *Your Hidden Light* in order to share with others what she believes is the most direct and efficient path to achieving

your desire
growth, and

Raana pl
the human
of self-reali
of developi
with a focu
purpose.

Raana
her two y
working, s
to beautif
everyday

CPSIA information can be obtained at www.ICGtesting.com
Printed in the USA
BVOW09s2354261217
503694BV00001B/13/P

Resources

Listed alphabetically by title:

Autobiography of a Yogi, Paramahansa Yogananda

Change Your Thoughts, Change Your life, Wayne Dyer

Conversations with God Book 1, 2, 3, Neale Donald Walsch

The Impersonal Life, Joseph Benner

Message from the Masters, Brian Weiss

Outwitting the Devil, Napoleon Hill

The Power of Now, Eckhart Tolle

The Secret, Rhonda Byrne

Secrets of the Millionaire Mind, T. Harv Eker

The Seven Spiritual Laws of Success, Deepak Chopra

Think and Grow Rich, Napoleon Hill

Please visit *www.yourhiddenlight.com* for additional resources.

About the Author

Raana Zia has spent her career holding executive level leadership roles in large Fortune 500 retail companies including the position of Chief Financial Officer. She has spent over 15 years developing leaders and coaching people and teams to maximize their abilities and achieve their goals in the corporate world. Her passion for personal and leadership development and an intense desire to discover her own purpose and potential led her down an unexpected path of self-realization and spirituality. Raana's journey into self-discovery opened her up to a greater understanding of her direct connection and influence over her reality. Her realizations and personal experiences compelled her to write *Your Hidden Light* in order to share with others what she believes is the most direct and efficient path to achieving your desires and living a life of happiness, continued growth, and fulfillment.

Raana plans to further pursue her passion for maximizing the human potential by being a spark in the movement of self-realization and empowerment. She is in the process of developing other books related to this subject matter with a focus on leadership development and fulfilling your purpose.

Raana currently lives in New Jersey with her husband, her two young children, and her dog. When she isn't working, she loves to snuggle and laugh with her kids, travel to beautiful places, eat great food, ski, and experience the everyday wonders and magic of the spiritual world.

For more information about Raana, go to
www.yourhiddenlight.com

CPSIA information can be obtained
at www.ICGtesting.com
Printed in the USA
BVOW09s2354261217
503694BV00001B/13/P